# SEMIOTICS AND FIELDWORK

**PETER K. MANNING**
*Michigan State University*

Qualitative Research Methods,
Volume 7

**SAGE** PUBLICATIONS
The Publishers of Professional Social Science
Newbury Park   Beverly Hills   London   New Delhi

*For information address:*

SAGE Publications, Inc.
2111 West Hillcrest Drive
Newbury Park, California 91320

SAGE Publications Inc.          SAGE Publications Ltd.
275 South Beverly Drive  28 Banner Street
Beverly Hills                   London EC1Y 8QE
California 90212                England

SAGE PUBLICATIONS India Pvt. Ltd.
M-32 Market
Greater Kailash I
New Delhi 110 048 India

International Standard Book Number 0-8039-2761-4
International Standard Book Number 0-8039-2640-5 (pbk.)

Library of Congress Catalog Card No. 87-042734

FIRST PRINTING

When citing a university paper, please use the proper form. Remember to cite the correct
Sage University Paper series title and include the paper number. One of the following
formats can be adapted (depending on the style manual used):

(1) IVERSEN, GUDMUND R. and NORPOTH, HELMUT (1976) "Analysis of
Variance." Sage University Paper series on Quantitative Applications in the Social
Sciences, 07-001. Beverly Hills: Sage Pubns.

*OR*

(2) Iversen, Gudmund R. and Norpoth, Helmut. 1976. *Analysis of Variance*. Sage
University Paper series on Quantitative Applications in the Social Sciences, series no.
07-001. Beverly Hills: Sage Pubns.

# C O N T E N T S

*For Esther Gibbard Manning*
*and*
*Kenneth G. Manning*

## EDITORS' INTRODUCTION

**Formal theoretical models** of social action are often disregarded by fieldworkers more intent on telling particulars than on making comparative generalities. Peter Manning, in this eighth monograph of the Qualitative Research Methods Series, brings recent linguistic and pragmatic approaches to the analysis of communication and meaning to bear on fieldwork traditions. From the perspective developed in this book, it is a fallacy to treat fieldwork and comparison as fundamentally distinct, one as descriptive and the other as theoretical. Fieldword requires both a theory of description and a method of comparison. One without the other is sterile. Professor Manning decries both the detailed "rustling-of-the-wind-in-the-palm-trees" kind of ethnography as well as the abstract social algebra of formal theory that so often seems to hold space, time, and people inside a sort of conceptual black hole.

*Semiotics*, the science of signs, offers fieldworkers a systematic guide in this respect. It is, however, a demanding taskmaster, for it challenges the fieldworker to formalize relationships uncovered in the live and moving worlds of message, discourse, text, and meaning. While there are serious reservations expressed with current formulations of the aims and methods of fieldwork in this book, Professor Manning provides a conciliatory touch and agenda. Rather than simply rooting out orthodoxy and attacking it from the perspective of the new, this monograph shows how conventional forms of fieldwork can be enriched and deepened by explicitly attending to matters of signification. Semiotics is of growing importance in the social sciences, and this is a book that demonstrates why.

*John Van Maanen*
*Marc L. Miller*

5

# PREFACE

**In my previous works** on policing, narcotics, police communications, and the forms and logic of disease, I argued for a degree of formalism, a logic of techniques, and a kind of cognitive sociology drawing on ideas of Aaron Cicourel, Harold Garfinkel, Erving Goffman, and Claude Lévi-Strauss. These were tentative and rather messy works in many ways, a combination of ideas, metaphors, tactics, and concepts. They drew eclectically upon various sources, as did those writers who most influenced my writings. In later works, especially (1980), and recent publications such as "Limits of the Semiotic Structuralist Perspective Upon Organizational Analysis" (1985), "Signwork" (1986b), "Texts as Echoes" (1986c), and *Signifying Calls* (forthcoming), the formalist mode and influence of Umberto Eco is evident. Less and less detail and fewer descriptions of persons, settings, narratives, emotion, and motion find their way into the text.

These matters are squeezed out by the power of formalistic approaches, those that seek to derive rules of thumb, inferential generalizations about procedures and practices, taxonomies, and paradigms and domains of thinking (metaphors and other associations among signs). This evolution is further demonstrated in this book. This neoformalism is accompanied by less and less interest in the study of emotion, sentiment, and the messy particulars of life as a sociological domain. Perhaps derivation of ordering principles, much like the enterprise at the heart of psychoanalysis itself, has both a calming and a clarifying consequence.

This book in many ways has less feeling hanging around the text, less emotion between the lines, fewer tales submerged or alluded to. It strives more for the tranquility that derives from insight, from flashes of explanation, and patches of lucidity. It claims more and says less.

It is also a book embedded in transatlantic movement and experience, and is suffused with time in Oxford and East Lansing, and marked by flights over the Atlantic (about 20 times in the last five years).

7

8

I would like to thank John Boal, Donald Harris, and Dick Markovits of the centre of Socio-Legal Studies; Wolfson College, Oxford, where I was a Visiting Fellow and later a Research Fellow; Sir Henry Fisher, former President of Wolfson College; Balliol College, where I was a Fellow during 1982-1983; and my chairs at Michigan State.

From time to time, comments on these ideas have been offered by John Van Maanen, Robert Cooper, and Norman Denzin.

I am very grateful for the efficient and effective typing of Roxie Damer and Tammy Argersinger at Michigan State.

In my oscillating movements across the Atlantic, I accumulated more debts than I shall ever be able to repay. I formulated these ideas in 1981-1986, and during this time, Elaine Player was my critic, friend, supporter, and my primary point of social reality. Others have acted on my behalf at critical points and I am very grateful to them: Jennifer Hunt, Ellen Greenman, Chris Vanderpool, and Bob Trojanowicz. Ellen's forbearance was not an afterthought and I thank her for both. Kerry, Merry, and Peter are the rock stars of my galaxy; and, as I wrote in 1977 and 1980, they have paid for these books in ways we recognize only vaguely.

*P. K. Manning*
East Lansing, Michigan

# INTRODUCTION

**This book provides a rationale** for the application of a formal method, semiotics, derived from linguistics and the science of signs more generally, to fieldwork in the social sciences. It is intended for an audience whose acquaintance with fieldwork and with semiotics as a method is limited. It also intends to provide a rationale for the use of such methods, for there are several sorts of methods derived from semiotics, in the social sciences more generally. The latter is of lesser importance than the former.

This title has two facets to it: *fieldwork*, defined as systematic gathering of data on specific aspects of social life by means other than social surveys, demographic techniques, and experimentation that includes an ongoing relationship with those studied, and *semiotics*, an approach to the analysis of social life that assumes that language is a model for other systems of signs and that seeks to identify the rules or principles that guide *signification* (the process by which objects in the world communicate meaning). The two facets derive from different traditions: Fieldwork is based upon pragmatism and symbolic interactionism and is associated with the emergence of sociology as a search for and understanding of societies and social worlds and the life histories contained therein. It is based upon inference and induction, and seeks to build up arguments from individual observations patterned by group relations or culture.

Semiotics, on the other hand, is derived from the rationalist tradition, draws upon structural (rule-based) explanations, and grew from the attempts of de Saussure (1966) to break from historical and static descriptive linguistics that dominated Europe in the late nineteenth century. It seeks to derive explanation of cases from general rules or principles (*abduction,* as Peirce termed it), and to discern and make obvious the underlying pattern, model, or order that obtains among various forms of communication such as music, art, literature, and formal scientific languages (see Culler, 1975).

The literatures that lie behind each of these aspects of the present volume are quite different as well. One is the classic literature of the "Chicago School" of American sociology, of anthropology, of modern fieldwork, and the large body of literature on qualitative methods more generally. The other is the literature of linguistics, of literature, of fields of philosophy concerned with semantics, implicature, pragmatics and symbolic logic, and writers in what Jameson (1972) calls the great formalist traditions (Marxism, Phenomenology, and linguistics). Historically, they stand, in some sense, in opposition to each other—the formal and informal, the rational and the empirical; the pragmatic and the formalist, the ahistorical and the historicist; the subjectivist and the objectivist. All such oppositions, this book intends to show, are false and misleading. They contain truth that can arise from exploring an apparent paradox. In another sense as well, this contrast is a function of the ways in which fieldwork has been defined in the past, and the somewhat narrow scope it has been given (see Adler and Adler, 1987). It need not be seen as being as restrictive as it has been; nor is semiotics, as the brilliant and inspirational writings of Umberto Eco (1979a, 1979b, 1984) show, restricted to precious and convoluted literary discourse among members of the French Academy.

Thus, the task of the book is to reduce some of the sharply drawn lines around disciplines and bodies of ideas, to provide examples of work that bridge the modes or approaches, and to show readers what sorts of problems are produced by such a perspectival shift.

The book begins with an outline of traditions of fieldwork, pointing out their assumptions, limits, and contributions to social sciences. This occupies Chapter 1. Chapter 2 again introduces the reader to semiotics, drawing on the works of Eco (1979a, 1979b, 1984), Culler (1975), and latterly the works of Barthes (1972), Goffman (1967, 1969, 1972, 1974, 1981) and related ideas drawn from pragmatists such as Levinson (1983), ethnomethodologists such as Cicourel (1973), Garfinkel (1967), and conversational analysts (Atkinson and Heritage, 1985). In Chapter 3, examples from fieldwork based on semiotic modes are summarized. Research on police communications and nuclear safety are presented. A final chapter outlines the limits of semiotics, and the kinds of problems that might be addressed using this approach. Some connections are drawn to the emerging formalisms of everyday life.

# 1. FIELDWORK AND ITS TRADITIONS

**Although fieldwork is often discussed** as a technique or method without serious diversity, as Douglas (1976), Adler and Adler (1987), and Needham (1984) have pointed out, it is, in fact, several interrelated modes of gathering materials. The three predominant modes of fieldwork, the "Chicago School," the anthropological mode identified with British social anthropology, and the phenomenological-existential will be discussed in the first section of this chapter. Closely related to this distinction are matters of fieldwork tactics and role-relations that have a profound affect on the data gathered and the analysis undertaken. These will be outlined in a second section of the chapter. Intertwined with the modes of fieldwork and the tactics of its implementation are the endemic issues of explanation (what is to be accounted for and to what purpose), reliability (are my findings reproducible and can they be confirmed by other investigators?), and validity (are the reported findings accurate and a true picture of the phenomenon?). As again, Douglas (1976), Needham (1984), and Johnson (1975) have repeatedly noted, these vexing issues have not been well addressed in fieldwork. A set of descriptive-analytic issues then arise and are discussed in the third section of the chapter. In a final section of the chapter, a more delimited and precise claim is made for fieldwork as a descriptive base for analysis. The domain in which it has its major utility is identified and the complementarity of semiotics is suggested. The last section will set out the strengths of semiotics in fieldwork, and intends to bridge the critical material in the previous sections with the following chapter, which advances a semiotic approach to fieldwork as well as a rationale for semiotic analysis of field data. Chapter 2 will be focused rather more than this upon semiotics as an analytic technique, providing a background for some examples of fieldwork using semiotics.

## Fieldwork Traditions

Three traditions or approaches to fieldwork can be identified. They are in no sense mutually exclusive, nor are their contributions to the

11

development of fieldwork equal. There is a chronological aspect to the order of discussion, but there are still many working British and continental anthropologists following the British tradition and there were earlier travelers who practiced a kind of close, feelings-based observation that resembles the existential approach flourishing today. In some sense, the great source of all fieldwork is the travelogue and the travel book, followed closely by the missionary and colonial tradition of keeping diaries, making observations, and collecting artifacts. Thus, the British tradition sets the model upon which much current fieldwork is based. The growth and development of large cities in both Europe and America was a second great stimulus to fieldwork, observation, and data-gathering as seen in the works of Mayhew, the Webbs, and Jane Adams.

The three also have key exemplars that are mentioned below. Among the most important in setting the tradition of British social anthropology were such writers as Malinowski (a Pole working at the London School of Economics), A. R. Radcliffe-Brown, Evans-Pritchard, and, later, Raymond Firth. The Chicago School, writing in the 1920s and 1930s in America, was composed loosely of Robert Park and students and associates such as W. I. Thomas and F. Znaniecki, Ernest Burgess, E. C. Hughes, and later Howard Becker and Erving Goffman. The third tradition is much less that than the others, more nascent, and perhaps only an important current variation. This group, called "existential" because of their interest in the fit among feelings, symbols, and behavior in given contexts, and the role of the observer in identifying with and empathizing with the observed, is composed of such people as Jack Douglas, John Johnson, and Patti and Peter Adler.

These traditions vary in the extent to which they raise questions about a semiotic approach to fieldwork analysis. Since the primary limitations of any fieldwork method are related not only to the method but to the aims and purposes of the research itself, the assumption is made that selection of the fieldwork approach is based upon a careful assessment of the aims of the research itself. Detailed discussions of these issues can be found elsewhere (Cicourel, 1964; Bruyn, 1966; Glaser and Strauss, 1967; McCall and Simmons, 1969; Lofland, 1976; Lofland and Lofland, 1983; Schatzman and Strauss, 1973; Douglas, 1976; Denzin, 1978; Schwartz and Jacobs, 1979; Emerson, 1983; Hammersley and Atkinson, 1983).

*(1) The British Anthropological Tradition.* As many have noted, the British fieldwork tradition grew from several sources, including the

empire and its administrative requirements, a knowledge base for decision making, and language and cultural knowledge for proper social comportment, and the British missionary and explorer tradition (see Manning, 1978, for a summary). The anthropologists were, therefore, by definition, nonmembers of the society, outsiders in culture, of lighter color, and certainly foreign. They could not be covert in their participation, and were often officially resident in the settings (see Gluckman, 1971). They were in a sense officially present, or at least known to be there for nonparticipant purposes, even when their roles involved deeper or more comprehensive involvement such as participation in religious, ceremonial, or everyday activities. The aim was in some way to penetrate the culture first by learning the language, often painfully en situ, then by being isolated and often unable to leave the setting in distant tribal worlds, learning the ways of life. There were physical, cultural, social, and personal reservations built into activities of this kind (Berreman, 1962). Perhaps a result of living for long periods of time with people was a practical requirement to understand the society as do members, and to be in some constant feedback-interaction mode with local peoples. Practical constraints also resulted in pressures for involvement of a physical as well as a psychological sort. Even the distance from "natives" displayed by people like Malinowski must in part be understood as a mode of coping with strong and constant pressures for involvement and incorporation (Wax, 1972; see Adler and Adler, 1987, on coping with pressures to become even further involved). This en situ observation tended to produce massive field notes about every imaginable detail of life, including drawing, craftwork, native documents, films, video- and audio tapes, pictures, diaries of the observer as well as others in the setting, interviews, and other written documents of other observers of the same group.

The proper attitude to such people is perhaps misunderstood by modern observers and equated with current concern for empathy and "being in touch with others" (an especially American sort of preoccupation). It is more perhaps the sort of detached sympathy that one might bring to teaching school rather than to understanding a loved one (see Wax, 1972). It was assumed that the tactic of being open to the groups— often isolated, small preliterate communities in Africa, in this case— would lead to mutual confidence and trust and that these, in turn, would combine to produce a context in which information about even the most intimate aspects of life would be shared between the researcher(s) and the people observed. One identified with one's people, area, and culture. (Even now, these are the primary sources of identity for many anthropologists, and one division of interests in an anthropology department.) In effect, cooperation and trust that extend into all areas of life is the model, and long-term identification with the people is assumed. Anthropologists' identification lies more with a people than with the discipline, theories of various kinds, or absolute truth (see Douglas on this point, 1976, p. 43).

Related to these notions are four rather important implications for the nature of anthropological theorizing and data analysis. Such a stance leads to a case-based, ethnocentric view, or what might be called an "emic" or internal perspective that is not general and is limited in its interpretative range to that observed culture (Berreman, 1966). This is complemented by, in British social anthropology, but not in all social anthropology, a close attention to empirical data, or the facts, rather than to more abstract questions of theory. With the possible exception of the study of kinship systems, British social anthropology has eschewed model-building or "grand theories" and favored close descriptions of small isolated social systems in distant places (see, for example, recent issues of the Royal Anthropological Society publication, *Man*). Since much of the work is undertaken alone, there is a degree of auto-didacticism inherent in this approach, as there is still in all forms of fieldwork. At best, it is in an apprenticeship that one learns the craft of fieldwork (see Epstein, 1967; Rock, 1979, ch. 6). The fundamental questions of comparatism are rarely raised (but see Needham, 1978, 1980, 1981, 1983). There is a continuing question: Is anthropology a scientific—even in the usual meaning of social scientific—discipline that seeks generalizable, cumulative knowledge in an objective fashion, or is it a literary craft, modeled on the writing style of Clifford Geertz (see Geertz, 1973, 1983)?

*(2) The Chicago and Neo-Chicago Traditions.* The separation between the anthropological and sociological approaches to fieldwork has been based on disciplinary training, and perhaps an affinity for nonurban fieldwork among anthropologists and urban fieldwork among sociologists. Even at the University of Chicago, the influences mingled (Park, 1973). The sociological fieldwork tradition was influenced at Chicago in the 1930s by Robert Redfield (1941, 1960), and later by W. Lloyd Warner, the author of the classic studies of stratification in America, The Yankee City series (1960), and by interest shown in Chicago in the growing urbanization of America, especially in the city of Chicago itself (Short, 1971, Park and Burgess, 1969/1921). There were

also strong influences of social meliorism, evangelical Protestantism, and social and political reform (see Davis, 1975, for an overview of these influences in early Chicago and the fieldwork tradition).

Early fieldworkers associated with the University of Chicago were somewhere between investigative reporters, travelers in exotic lands, and casual comparativists (see Douglas, 1976, ch. 1). They were in some cases former or current members of the social groups they studied; Park wrote about the news and news reporting; Znaniecki, a Pole of upper-class birth, studied the adaptation of the Poles to Chicago; Anderson studied hobos and had been one. In other words, *membership* preceded the analysis in many cases. In another sense, there was an attempt to be a covert or at least marginally participant member stepping back to look with new eyes at something about which one previously knew (Hughes, 1971, ch. 43). Some roles were as mere observers or involved partial participation, while some took an observer role entirely. The extent of their immersion in the culture, and indeed the extensiveness of the chosen problem, also varied, even when they attempted to examine the culture or the social group in some broad context. In many respects, the aim of Chicago-style fieldwork was, and still is, to penetrate a culture that was partially known already to the observer, or was embedded in a well-known culture. Thus the fieldwork of Whyte (1943/1955) on a Boston Italian neighborhood, or Suttles (1968) on a Chicago ethnic neighborhood, were exercises in partial cultural understanding in an already known context, that is, American, urban, ethnically diverse settings. Most of the problematic issues attendant in the British tradition were obviated here insofar as the language, the culture (to some extent), and the setting were partially known, and the isolation substantially less. There was, in short, less need to understand and cope with the environment as did the "natives." Some fieldworkers, as is still the case, commuted, or had homes away from the sites in which they worked. Thus psychological and physical distance from one's home rarely existed, and certainly not in to the extent found in classic anthropological fieldwork. The problems, as discussed below, were in maintaining one's "limbo" status, or marginality, rather than the opposite.

The data gathered in the Chicago tradition tend to be less diverse and perhaps less full in character for the reasons outlined above (more was, in fact, already known), as well as because the problem focus was narrower and more likely to have been defined in advance, for example, the career of the juvenile delinquent (Shaw, 1930/1966, 1931), the nature of the gang (Thrasher, 1927), and, later, on such topics as the moral career of the mental patient (Goffman, 1961) and of a physician (Becker, Geer, Hughes, and Strauss, 1961).

The proper attitude was one of a "limbo member," or a "marginal man," someone who understands and empathizes with the group under study, but who retains an alternative perspective. Something of a binocular vision is required. There was the overall aim of creating an empathetic understanding of the unfolding nature of the cultural life of the group, mainly focused on a small segment, and with the purpose of maintaining a role (either fully participant through to fully observer) throughout the course of the study.

Tactically, as was the case in the British tradition, one was to approach the group openly, and seek to inspire trust and confidence through this open approach to one's subject population (Wax, 1952). This openness was expected to be reciprocated. The insider's knowledge of the social world would, in fact, be partial, and reported as such; there was no assumption, interest, or belief in the idea that one would reveal to outsiders aspects of the society that were destructive to the group studied. This, of course, is consistent with the study of the powerless, "underdogs," with whom researchers identified, and consistent with many of the traditions of social science that debunk, or treat ironically, the powerful groups in society (Becker, 1970). For these powerful groups, the rules of discretion are modified if and when such studies are carried out at all (Dalton, 1959; Hunter, 1960).

The potential for generalized explanation within the Chicago style of fieldwork is considerable. The theoretic assumptions of the work, based on theories of social disorganization (Davis, 1975), the ecological-zone theory of social and cultural differentiation and growth (Park and Burgess, 1921/1969), and the social-psychological perspective of symbolic interactionism developed by Mead, Park, and, later, Blumer (1969), were the tacit, if not explicit context within which the problems were found, studied, and published (Becker, 1970). Although in many respects the level of generalization was modest, there were continuous attempts to integrate the studies into a social ecological framework (Short, 1971), the framework of work and occupations (Hughes, 1971), and of collective behavior (Becker, 1982). However, the oral tradition of passing on the ideas from one to another verbally, the apprenticeship and craftlike basis for fieldwork (Junker, 1960; Rock, 1979), and the lack of comparative method (either of other groups or of other cultures, although this was implicit in the Chicago work) hampered theory-building and formalization.

_(3) The Existential Tradition._ Recent work by Douglas and students, published in several volumes, suggests that a third, very contemporary, variant on the first two models of fieldwork is now emerging (see J. Douglas, 1967, 1971, 1976; Adler, 1985; Adler and Adler, 1987; Johnson, 1975; Kotarba and Fontana, 1984; Altheide, 1976; Douglas and Johnson, 1977). The source of the work is Californian mythology about the nature of trust, experience, life-style, truth, and culture. The studies done of California, as Matza (1969) had noted in the late 1960s, a result of the neo-Chicagoan influence that followed the move of Blumer to Berkeley in the late 1950s, affects the discipline in important ways. California is, of course, a zero-point culture, because no one belongs, there is no "native culture," and virtually everyone engaged in the studies is a non-Californian. So, for example, all the key persons in the tradition come from outside: the Adlers from New York, Douglas from the South, Johnson and Kotarba from the Midwest. Their neo-marginality was that of virtually all other Californians: identity and self must be negotiated in a zero-base culture. Their roles and participation were total in some sense as the variants upon Californian life—the massage parlor, the nude beaches, the drug dealing—the new life-styles of the area were available to everyone. No special skills, talents, training, knowledge, or other background equipment were needed; one was one of them. One was not isolated, not in a strange world in absolute terms, and the search for identity was not constituted by stepping back from what one might have been or was, but in understanding the meaning of one's being at that moment.

The pressures were of a social and psychological sort. The society in which one moved could not be assumed to be cooperative or consensual (Douglas, 1976, ch. 3); it was certainly not a society of cooperative subjects at any level other than the most superficial, and the perspectives of members could not easily be replicated by a close understanding of the views of a handful of key informants. The view was as Douglas (1976) summarized in a striking paragraph from his agenda for the new fieldwork in _Investigative Social Research_. This manifesto is the only new statement of fieldwork since the height of the influence of the Chicago school in the 1930s:

> This basic approach assumes there is a necessary interdependency between the nature of the social world we wish to study and the specific methods we should use to study that social world. (One would say in philosophical terms that ontology and epistemology are necessarily interdependent.) Our basic, largely common-sensical view of what the

social world is like is of basic importance in deciding to get more truth about that world, and what methods to use in getting it. This means that we must deal continually with what the social world is really like and show how the methods are related to that social world. It means as well that when we have different goals of truth, different kinds of data we want to achieve, we want to use different methods to get there.

The result of this definition of the task meant that the constraints were no longer cultural, physical, linguistic, or, even in some sense, social. They were preeminently existential or psychological; matters of meaning or of understanding internal states (see Douglas, 1976, p. 35, note 1; Adler and Adler, 1987). Whereas for Malinowski and associates and the Chicago school of fieldwork, the issues were matters of finding and flatly stating objective truth, the issues for the existential field-workers devolve from the researchers' stance to the world and the transactional relationship between the subject and the object (see Thomas, 1983). How does one know? What can be known? What sorts of knowing are there? The needed distance in the field was stated in a set of tactics for the maintenance of the fluid, developing, dynamic roles of both the participants and the observers themselves (Douglas, 1976, chs. 4-8). Field notes and modes of keeping them became secondary or tertiary issues, rarely discussed in detail in any of the classic sources, nor in those in the existential tradition; it is *there* as an issue, but seems to be relegated in the published work to questioning of relationship and meaning.

The proper attitude, which Adler and Adler (1987) discuss in depth, is in dialectical relationship to the attitude of distant appreciation found in earlier traditions. They do not fear involvement, but encourage it. Roles change, settings change, groups change, feelings change, and one understands these changes as a part of the fieldwork context. The question is not one of involvement, but the relationship between the kinds of involvement, the kinds of truth sought, and the sort of problem one is studying. The Adlers and Douglas are concerned with such questions in their studies. In their analyses of drug dealing, nude beaches, and beauty, they address questions of misinformation, lies, deceptions, fronts, evasions, and how to deal with taken-for-granted meanings (the issue is to recognize what one knows in the same way others know it, not what one does not know as in the case of isolated preliterate groups), problematic meanings, and self-deceptions (chs. 4 and 5 of *Investigative Social Research*). There is no assumption here of consensus, of cooperative subjects, or of a single unifying perspective; quite the contrary. The overall aim is to penetrate and reduce the social facades of others using the strategic and tactical weapons of intellectuals. Thus the older rules about secrecy, trust and mutual trust, protection of one's subjects' worlds, and, even to some extent, the editing of field reports to save the face of the researcher and the research subjects, no longer hold.

The aim of such fieldwork is to develop a view of truth, or, more properly, a view of the nature of human feeling, and as such it claims generality beyond the beaches of Southern California or the fern bars of Sausalito. Douglas claims it has cross-species validity. There are no grand theories, but the devotion to both symbolic interaction and existentialism provides a link to such broad ideas as the self, symbols, feelings, and the interactional social psychology of Erving Goffman. Importantly, this work has been team work, and has sought to make the conditions of analysis as well as data-gathering group based rather than individually based. The diffusion of identity and questions of meaning are group questions. In a brilliant example of this sort of fieldwork, Peter and Patricia Adler worked as a team to study drug dealing and smuggling in Southern California (see Adler, 1985). They maintained a close relationship with their informants, including loans, socializing, mutual favors, in part a consequence of living in close proximity. (This research began after the Adlers moved into their home and it grew from that, rather than from their finding a research topic and moving to the setting temporarily to study it.) They effectively demonstrate aspects of Southern Californian life in their research. As I wrote elsewhere:

The existential theme of the last chapter is well foreshadowed. The fast life is seen above all as fun. "Primary to the fast life was abundant drug consumption, generating intense pleasures. They wanted these now and for all time, not ten years from now when their investments or pension plans matured" [p. 50]. Their rational business practices were ironic in this light, "it was their very quest for unmitigated decadence which caused them to impose rational constraints on their existence" [p. 151]. She continues: "Dealers and smugglers, above all else, pursued deviance to live freely and wildly, to make their hedonistic way of life possible." They are rational in spite of their passionate and irrational drives; and as Adler notes, they are rationally organized in spite of the fact that they are not rationally organized people [p. 149]. They react against the bureaucratic, staid and constraining aspects of modern life. The combination of routine and risk manifested by these modern traders is a rather interesting variant on Weberian capitalism and its spirit: they disconnect the material and the rational, and by maximizing short-run rationality, something like the booty capitalists described by Weber, they determined their failure [Manning, 1986a].

In these three traditions, still flourishing and contributing to knowledge, one can see the strengths and weaknesses of fieldwork. Fieldwork has developed for understanding problems that require close observation of individuals in interaction around key issues of life, death, and transition, where one requires knowledge of detail and nuance unavailable otherwise, and where control of the relevant variables affecting such matters is neither possible, understood, nor desirable at this level of the development of knowledge. As Douglas (1976, ch. 2) points out, there are a variety of approaches to social knowledge, and fieldwork is a close version of natural observation of everyday life using somewhat more refined tools such as diaries, interviews, field notes, and levels of participation (either nonparticipant such as in-depth interviewing or discussions, or participation at various levels, which is the mode of the three traditions reviewed here). The goals of social research that seek situated meanings of individuals such as life histories; careers; multiperspectival research that attempts to fit together various lines of interpretation, for example, that of the drug user and drug police, the regulated as well as the regulator; or that attempts to produce representation of meaning at a group level will all require some investigative fieldwork.

The emergence of various traditions in fieldwork, including a movement in the direction of more formalization of investigations in the field such as ethnoscience (see Agar, this series, 1985; Manning and Fabrega, 1976; Tyler, 1969) all attempt to cope with the limitations of fieldwork. To a remarkable degree, the problems are seen as strategic and tactical, or partial attempts to control questions of access to settings, maintaining trust and openness, role relations in the field, tactical and strategic problems of obtaining data, and interpersonal and personal ethical and psychological problems. Some attention is given in other literature on fieldwork to the questions of reliability and validity (McCall and Simmons, 1969), specific tactics such as observation and the ethnographic interview (Spradley, 1979, 1980), gender issues in fieldwork (Warren and Rassmussen, 1977), and broader fit between methods and settings (Van Maanen, 1983; Van Maanen, Dabbs, and Faulkner, 1984). Some challenges to traditional modes of fieldwork have also been mounted by ethnomethodologists studying work in laboratories (Lynch; 1985, Knorr-Cetina, 1981; Pickering, 1985; Woolgar and LaTour, 1979). Assumptions about gathering members' meanings is challenged; these researchers argue that sociologists obscure issues by overlaying sociological or secondary concepts upon everyday reasoning and thinking based on the natural attitude (see Adler and Adler, 1987; Douglas, 1976; as well as Mehan and Wood, 1975; Leiter, 1980; Handel, 1982; Heritage, 1985). In an odd sense, they are arguing for more universal features of everyday reasoning—talk and discourse, more generally—that bring them in closer line with the semiological tradition than some might imagine (see below as well as Boon, 1982). Other questions raised by neo-structuralists in anthropology (Boon, 1982), comparativists such as Needham (1984, Manning, 1985b), and by Marxists (Godelier, 1977) are not addressed here. They are asking questions that in part are addressed by the following material on fieldwork, as well as by raising the broader political and social role of social science in social and economic development, and the diffusion of knowledge. The focus here is upon the relationship between field method, the analysis of data, and codification of derived knowledge.

Some fieldwork has emerged now as an art form of sorts in which the naturalistic detailed description of a culture is sought to be rendered as natives see it; express it to themselves; symbolize it in diverse modes (verbal, nonverbal, material, and written); and behave in accord with these understandings. Fieldwork in this style is reflexive. It attempts to render a culture for readers as do natives. The fieldworker thus stands as a kind of interpreter midway between the natives and the readers, and tries to express the culture of one in terms of the other. As Van Maanen (in press) has shown, the voice one uses in presenting one's findings and in making truth claims is an intimate feature of the art form itself. The major contributions have been in describing parts of the world unknown to others, especially their beliefs, religions, values, norms, attitudes, and practices. Their descriptions are often implicitly contrasting conceptions laid out against a backdrop of unexplicated knowledge that the reader brings to the description. We see cultures against what we know about our own. The major institutions of medicine, law, religion, and science provide clear and obvious contrasts, but is unclear often whether there is a moral judgment made about the efficiency, efficacy, or propriety of these practices (see Needham, 1984). In medical anthropology, for example, it is clear that the bias, except for healing by belief, is in the direction of Western biomedicine (Fabrega, 1974). These descriptions, as Geertz (1973, 1983) has so often argued, aim in some sense to be broadly educative, raising the level of awareness of people much as did DeToqueville, Martineau, or Lafcadio Hearn (see also Fussell, 1980).

The rare controversies within anthropology that can be identified, such as the utility of various forms of kinship models, illustrate that the level of systematic knowledge is insufficient in either anthropology or sociology to create disputes about priority, validity, or refutation of a hypothesis. Much more attention, as we have seen, seems devoted to seeking understanding of the role of the self and meaning in relation to the group studied. Some traditions focus more upon the researcher and his or her feelings, roles, and ethics than others, while some focus more on the constitution of the researched group, and the role and self of the researcher fade into the background. Ironically, the self of the researcher is the instrument of the research, but is nevertheless only recently the object of considerable writing in the fieldwork literature. This is because perhaps, as Douglas (1976) and Johnson (1975) have pointed out, a notion of objective truth taken from the natural sciences is used in fieldwork as the basis for judging the adequacy of findings. This is one among many contradictions in the fieldwork traditions.

## Limitations of Fieldwork

There are some important limitations of any fieldwork approach, given the stated aims and purposes of such research. Clearly, fieldwork is not suited for many sorts of problems, and is not used to undertake studies of them. Within the types of problems well-suited to fieldwork, a series of limitations remain.

*(1) Ad Hoc Problem Selection.* Most studies based on fieldwork provide what might be called a "near-version" of the problem-selection on the basis of process. That is, they rationalize their problem-selection on the basis of recognized standards, accounts, or acceptable nature of their initial contact with the circumstance that they later studied. For example, my first writing in the police field came as a result of being asked to write a chapter that Egon Bittner declined to write. This later led to work in England with the Metropolitan Police, which, in turn, was a result of the fact that my wife and I had wanted but could not manage a honeymoon in England and decided to go at the first opportunity: my first sabbatical leave. This pattern of accepting available opportunities for study, falling into a research problem,

23

pursuing a likely access, or following where the money leads is not likely to lead to systematic pursuit of intellectually or theoretically formulated questions and problems. Even if one grants that one should begin with the problematics of everyday life, and that one should be open and pursue them, the question arises: Why choose one rather than another problem for investigation? Because the selection of problems is neither theory- nor method-driven; cumulative knowledge available in virtually any area is limited. When continuity is visible, such as in the studies of Collier, Vogt, and Wasserman in Chiapas, of Redfield and Lewis in Tepotzlan, controversies arise. The first issue is, then, how problems are selected for study and what guides the choice of critical studies?

*(2) Limited Domain of Analysis.* There is an irony in field studies for, insofar as they focus on a narrow domain of culturally articulated knowledge, such as firewood (Metzger and Williams, 1966), marriage ceremonies (Metzger and Williams, 1963), terms of address (Brown and Ford, 1961), or types of ulceration (Frake, 1961), they are linked to the broader cultural and social setting only in the most circumscribed terms. The cultural knowledge is sufficient to permit one to locate the culture in time and space and in some cultural area, but rarely more than that. Most ethnographic studies provide a kind of précis of the culture and setting in a few paragraphs and then proceed to more detailed analyses. (See any issue of *Man, Ethnology,* or the *American Anthropologist.*) If, on the other hand, a general gloss on the culture is attempted, and this is only possible in small communities in any case, the analysis is necessarily very general. Because, as was pointed out above, with the exception of a few long-standing projects such as the Harvard-Stanford-Cornell Chiapas project (see Vogt, 1969, 1976), and the Chicago studies in the 1930s, there is no attempt to order and articulate projects even in the same cultural area. Studies tend to be done by young investigators, often Ph.D. students, on their own. By virtue of this, and the increasingly narrow definition of the Ph.D. dissertation, rather narrow and circumscribed problems are chosen for investigation. The combination of ad hoc problem selection and narrowness of focus based on the single investigator model produces studies unlikely to contribute to a body of knowledge addressing theoretically selected and analyzed problems.

*(3) Role Relationships Are Not Consistent.* Field studies, as the above review illustrates, are not based upon consistent definitions of the

role of the fieldworker. Some are overt, some covert; some are based on intense participation, some on very limited participation; some studies are systematically reflective and self-reflective, others are not; some rely importantly on key informants, while others are surveys; some studies are based on long-term relationships over virtually a lifetime, such as the studies of Raymond Firth in Tikopia, but most are single studies carried out in settings to which the researcher never returns (see Manning and Fabrega, 1976). Regardless of one's model of truth or knowledge, it is very difficult to compare these studies. Because self and role of the observer mediate the data gathered, information on the role of the observer is essential to questions of reliability and validity, or even of coherence of an explanatory framework. Insofar as the reflective relationship is critical to the enterprise, and that itself is unstandardized, there can be no more than moments, segments of social life, described, and a humanistic perspective displayed (Bruyn, 1966).

*(4) Descriptive Focus*. The primary rationale for field studies is that they describe a segment of the social world in some detail (see, for example, Lofland, 1976). Textbooks that provide an outline of procedures for analysis urge listing of types, instances of taxonomies and other low-level organization of data (Lofland, 1976, 1984). Manuals of theorizing from field data are organized around fairly discrete concepts and on organizing of field notes (Glaser and Strauss, 1967). Major journals in the field such as *Urban Life* and *Qualitative Sociology* are full of carefully done studies of discrete and bounded urban social worlds, such as pornographic book shops, soap operas, C.B. radio operators, and police lying, and are unconnected to general problems of the field. To some extent, this is a needed enterprise. Sociology relies upon tacit notions about the social organization of social life on an ad hoc basis without a clear understanding of social processes. Studies of mobility, for example, simply reduce it to movements from one occupational category to another without an understanding of the cognitive processes of evaluation, self-esteem, or self-investment that make social the process of job changing (compare Faunce, 1984). In the case of most papers in the leading journals of the field, methodology rather than theoretic questions make the work coherent; in qualitative journals such as *Urban Life*, it is the setting-specific findings gathered through field methods that organize the articles.

*(5) Single Case Focus*. The tradition of fieldwork, tied as it is to naturalistic and process explanations, has meant that most of the

published works are only implicitly comparative. Most are single case studies and, if they are done in complex urban societies, analyze only a small segment of some larger social system. They either make no claims to generality or their generality remains implicit. In the absence of specific dimensions along which some phenomena are being compared, it is difficult to establish the generality of the findings. The claimed presence or absence of something such as strategies for managing a "squat" (Kearns, 1981), clandestine sex (Lilly and Ball, 1981), aging (Unruh, 1985), or idealism (Haas and Shaffer, 1984) can be understood only against some distribution of such things in other occupations, societies, or cultures.[1]

The previous brief and perhaps rather too succinct review of three fieldwork traditions, and some of their preoccupations, origins, and aims, was a basis for a more critical examination of the limitations inherent to better appreciate the utility of the semiotic approach described in the following chapter and exemplified in Chapter 3. Inevitably, such a gloss on fieldwork and its many traditions is too broad, and the limitations presented overstated. However, the aim of this book is to present these matters as background against which the strengths and weaknesses of semiotics can be assessed rather than as a full picture of the traditions.

## NOTE

1. This is a random assortment. There is no intention to draw invidious connotations, or, indeed, to cast any reflections upon the quality of these well-written articles.

## 2. SEMIOTICS

Semiotics is primarily a mode of analysis that seeks to understand how signs perform or convey meaning in context. Although semiotics has been associated with rather precious topics and debates, it is inherently practical in the same sense that knowing a language is essential to displaying cultural competence. $H_2O$ stands for water, Uncle Sam for the United States, and the Crown for the head of the British State, yet all is understood without reflection because mental links are made between the signifier ($H_2O$) and the signified (water). It is this work that is to be explored in this book.

The work of semiotics is, as was suggested, to uncover the *rules* that govern the conventions of signification, whether these be in kinship, etiquette, mathematics, or art. It is not a descriptive technique that aims to lay out the historical or prior conditions necessary or sufficient for the appearance of a phenomenon (Brown, 1963; Manning, 1982a; Cressey, 1953). Nor does it seek to describe the motives of individual actors who animate social life, nor indeed has it any concern for individuals, their morals, attitudes, values, or behaviors except as they are symbolized within a system of signs.

Its formal and analytic character directs attention to signs and how they signify, both the association among a *series* or set of signs (such as a menu, list, traffic signs, or a course syllabus) and between a *signifier* (such as a traffic sign) and a *signified* (stop; go; no left turn). Because in every sense the system precedes the individual signs, and their associations and functions, attention is directed in the first instance to sign systems themselves as systems. The purpose is then to make formal the discerned relationships. Prior to a systematic discussion of the nature of sign systems and their analysis, consider a number of examples of signs in everyday life, and their functions and effects.

In chemistry and mathematics, signs such as $2 + 2 = 4$, or $H_2 SO_4$ are logically related one to another by known conventions, and the form of the relationship between signs is consistent from one formula to the next. The form of the relationships between the signs also represents the order of such matters in nature; there is a fit between their logic and the epistemological structure of the world. Another way to say this is that the physical world is organized by a known set of forces, elements, and dynamics, and formal systems of reasoning can analogically represent this.

In social life, codes and signs communicate social meanings that present complex problems of interpretative understanding. First, the signs that are used in everyday life communicate both *logical* relations (the snake is six inches from your hand) as well as *emotional* relations (THE SNAKE IS SIX INCHES FROM YOUR HAND!!!!!!!!!!!!!). These are sometimes confused and confusing, for the wrong affect may be brought to a logical problem as often as the wrong logic may be brought to an emotional problem. Second, language, which is used as the model for the analysis of signs systems more generally, whether one is speaking of traffic signs, Morse code, chemical formula, kinship systems, or etiquette, is doubly articulated. We use language to express ourselves and to express thought about language itself ("I told you a lie

last night"; the lie is a communication about a previous communication).
In formal systems such as law or even sociology, we may speak of double
articulation in the sense that sociology is a set of rules of thumb about
human behavior that are widely known ("interaction in families is more
frequent than outside families for young children"), as well as communication about those relationships ("this is characteristic of primary
groups").

Signs indicate groups and social relations. *Social signs* point to group
identity, to membership, and to social roles. Guiraud (1975, pp. 84-90)
provides a brief list of social signs: coats of arms, flags, totems, uniforms
(signs of group membership); insignia and decorations (which are
vestiges of the above); tatoos, make-up, hair styles (signs of fashion);
nicknames (individual identities as well as group identities); commercial
signs (functions of businesses and social areas); trademarks and logos
(the origins of a commodity). There are also signs of polite behavior
such as tone of voice and greetings (whether negative or positive);
nonverbal signs such as gestures or postures (a wave, a turn of the back);
spatial-temporal relations (how close are people to each other, when and
where?); and food (the order of eating, as well as the mode of
preparation, and style of serving all communicate). These do not on
their own signify anything, but may variously communicate to groups
and thus have a social reality, or they may divide groups (passing a
"joint" is seen as convivial in some groups, and as alienating among
others).

Social *codes* are integrated systems of signs. There are many of them,
but think, for example, of protocols or etiquette whose function it is to
communicate relations among individuals; rituals, where the group
itself is honored by its members; fashion, which is stylized communication of a social identity or role; and games, which represent in
microcosm larger social paradoxes, conflicts, and situations. All of
these are segments of sign-ordered behavior that one honors, often
without overt thought, but that are nevertheless arbitrary, selected,
reinforced by other customs and beliefs, and ordered as is language
itself.

Social signs, since they communicate group relations, have differing
capacities to represent social power, coercion, and shared meaning to
groups. Those signs that are hyperelevated into matters of trust, and
shared reality that approaches the unquestioned, are myths. (This is
discussed below.) For example, Barthes (1972) has offered the example
of the mythical role of wine for the French, but one might consider the

mythological role of tea for the British. (I paraphrase Barthes and use my own English experience.) To believe in tea is to affirm of one's location both by choice and without thinking in a British collective or group. To eschew or offer distance from tea is to expose oneself to having to explain why repeatedly. This attitude is neither understood nor accepted as normal. Knowing how to prepare tea (putting leaves in the pot, using a strainer to pour out the tea into the cups, putting the milk in first, serving tea on a tray with biscuits), how to drink it (slowly in cups, in longer drafts in mugs), how to share tea time with others, and how to tidy the cups is assumed to be common knowledge, signs of sociability, of competence, and good manners. Tea is a central part of society; it provides a basis both for morality and for an environment in which it is displayed. It is an ornament of the slightest ceremonials: from a brief gathering of two people to a very large gathering where afternoon refreshments are served. (Coffee is a morning drink and taken after meals among middle-class people.) Tea is for all weather (it cools and refreshes in the heat—above 60 degrees in England—and warms in the cold) and for all conditions (when hungry, it eases the unease; when thirsty, it quenches the thirst; when uneasy, it relaxes; when relaxed, it mobilizes and prepares; at night, in the form of a night drink, it soothes and calms and prepares one for deep sleep; in the morning, it stimulates and clears one's thoughts and prepares one for the rigors of the day ahead; and so on). It is, in short, deeply a part of British life. Parallels with other drugs are obvious, perhaps, but the most common commodities and substances serving these functions are automobiles, soft drinks, and beer in American advertising. In everyday life, there is far more diversity in what people buy, drink, and eat, and what they feel about them, but advertising, more than anything, is the production and reification of taste that then serves as a myth of unity in American Society.

In these examples illustrating five aspects of signs, their relation to each other and the physical and social world, their articulation, some of their social functions, their degree of integration and mythological aspects, is found a brief overview of the role of signs in social life.

In order to examine the general orientation of this volume to semiotics as well as to fieldwork, this chapter will include in the next section an outline of the aim of semiotics, its central concepts, and some aspects of context, change, and textual analysis. This will provide the basis for the third chapter, which identifies several of the issues that semiotics raises about sociological analysis using fieldwork, and

*[handwritten marginalia: traffic - way of getting there need rules speech]*

provides several examples of semiological analysis drawn from my work.

## The Orientation of Semiotics

Semiotics, as suggested above, is an orientation to the analysis of signs and signs about signs. There are several important aspects of the orientation, or the point of view itself. Semiotics is a formal mode of analysis that seeks principles and rules that account for a known pattern. It also is a form of cultural analysis. All human behavior, once interpreted, is conduct. Semiotics looks at rules that govern conduct. Semiotics distinguishes performance or *speech* from the rules that govern it or control speech, *language* rules. The language rules, like traffic rules, provide ways to get there, or to express "thought." If one wants to express a simple thought, such as "It is hot," it can be said at length with elaborate structure, full of adjectives and adverbs, and from the perspective of several people: "It was said on the weather report"; Uncle Joe said "that it will be hot"; and "I heard on the street that the neighbors think it is about 90." It can be simply expressed. In the same way that on any university campus there are several ways to drive between buildings, some rules about side of the road, stop signs and lights, and speed limits, there are several ways to express a thought.

Semiotics pulls itself in two separate directions: one in the direction of the study of the rules themselves, or *language,* and the other, the relationships between the language and performance or the consequences of speech acts, *pragmatics* (Levinson, 1983). In the study of rules or forms of language, attention is given only to the relations among the units that convey meaning. For example, think of a table setting. This is governed by rules about placement: fork(s) on the left of the plate, knife and spoon(s) on the right with the napkin. Extra spoons in England are laid across the top of the plate, and they may be either soup (very large) or sweet (smaller large) spoons. This is a form in which the positioning of the items is given by cultural rules; because we know this, we can laugh at mistaken settings, correct errors, or add needed implements if they are missing. We still understand an item's functions whether it is there or not, although these are indeed different knives, forks, and spoons encountered in homes, restaurants, or dining halls. We can use the item in other ways, such as using the knife as a screwdriver, or a spoon as a musical instrument, but that function is in a different *context* of meaning. To study the *form* of table setting and how

30

the items are given meaning is like studying the rules governing kinship, or organizational communication, or university grading. Looking at practices introduces pragmatics, applications of signs to conduct.

The *model of language* is used as a paradigm for all other sign systems. This is a contentious point to which we return. Is linguistics the model for all other social sciences—anthropology, sociology, psychology? Is language the model for all other nonverbal sign systems? Do we think about fashion, manners, and music in the same way(s) that we think about language? Is there some "deep structure" that allows us to understand music in poetic terms, to think about experience as if it were a play or work of art? There are some obvious parallels such as the singing of a poem, the critical notes describing music on a program, verbal descriptions of works of art found in museums, and the like. Can we extend this further and suggest that we can think about one thing in terms of another, making easy transformations of one into the other? Is a list of Big Ten football teams, ranked from one to ten, equivalent to the relative courage of each of the teams? First: courageous beyond belief, second: very courageous, third: somewhat courageous . . . down to eighth: cowardly; ninth: pusillanimous; and ten: unthinkable? Could this then be translated to the symbols for the teams? If Michigan State is first, University of Michigan second, Minnesota third, and, say, Northwestern ninth and Iowa tenth, does that mean that Spartans are more courageous than Wolverines, Wolverines more courageous than Gophers, Gophers much more courageous than Wildcats, and Wildcats more courageous than Hawkeyes? The point is that this is *thinking with* semiotics, looking at one system, finding its units and meanings, and then translating that system onto another one. It is thinking with one scheme about another one and moving back and forth.

Semiotics, like linguistics, studies wholes ordered by rules. The connection between sociology and linguistics comes insofar as both study the whole, or society, by the study of language or discourse:

Discourse becomes the proper topic of the human sciences because it is the one distinctively human product which operates at the boundaries between the cultural and the natural, that most crucial of nineteenth century distinctions. Discourse relies always on noncultural material and natural (bodily) supports (or, *signifiers*: phonetic signals, graphic marks) to produce cultural ideas (*signifieds*). Thus, from the structuralist view of language, the human sciences cannot idealize people as the strictly human, cultural, meaning-producing center of social life. Accordingly, the universality of discourse reminds us that we are actually a decentered product of both material and ideal, both natural and cultural factors. (Here one detects the influence of Marx on structuralist thought) [Lemert, 1979b, p. 100].

This preference for wholes, structures, or forms means that semiotics is *de-centered* in the sense that language provides the roles or voices with which one speaks (Lemert, 1979a). If one conceives of past social science as assuming the reality and centrality of individual actors, selves, and even embodied persons, structuralism is decentered in that it sees the codes, roles, perspectives, and structure of language as the ultimate reality. The human being is not the primary object in itself, a source of motivations, actions, or the basis from which one infers prior principles; the human being is constituted from and by discourse. In this sense, discourse and rules that govern it are seen as governing the possible forms, roles, and actions that one might imagine or impute to a "person." Persons attain status only as elements of a signifying system (Lemert, 1979b, p. 100). Thus semioticians might see a person as Freudians do, a bundle of symptoms ("a neurotic"), as a set of economic drives for consumption and production, as a chaos of passions as in a Judith Krantz novel, or a disembodied voice as do record producers. These are human constructions of humans, abstractions, and they make social life possible. By radically questioning the other aspects of humanity, and reducing human beings to objects constructed with a system of signs, structuralists want to show how much thinking produces social reality as well as how social reality creates thinking. Likewise, sociology treads a thin line between a structural discipline that examines only roles, norms, beliefs, systems, and groups, and a social psychological discipline that encompasses the subjective and individual (although these are not incompatible with a sociological frame of reference).

Interpretation is fundamental: Any system of rules, or forms, will have gaps, indeterminacies, and interpretative aspects. Think, for example, of a police uniform as a system of signs: each part, the hat, the jacket, the shirt and tie, the trousers, the shoes, the belt and tools (gun, radio, ammunition, truncheon), is distinctive, but takes its effect from the whole ensemble. They work by contrast; by what is not carried or worn. Distinctions within the police are based on what is not worn as well as what is, hence detectives are "out of the bag" (uniform), do not wear radios, truncheons, or large holstered weapons. They also can be a field for indeterminacy as when uniform officers wear Baseball caps and blue overblouses on warrant-serving raids. The cap contrasts with the uniform cap, and the overblouse with the uniform jacket, but the rest of the uniform remains the same. What is being communicated by this slight alteration: how is warrant serving like (and unlike) a baseball game? Does the jacket communicate to the citizen, the audience for this communication? Since all formal systems contain the sender and the receiver of the signs—as well as the message the channel used and the style of its communication—interpretation and indeterminancy are always a part of any display of signs. Eco suggests that that is where analysis begins:

> Semiotics must proceed to isolate structures *as if* a definite general structure existed; but to be able to do this, one must assume that this global structure is simply a regulative hypothesis, and that *every time a structure is described something occurs within the universe of signification which no longer makes it completely* reliable.

> But this condition of imbalance and apparent lack of stability puts semiotics on a par with other disciplines such as physics, governed—as this latter is—by such a methodological criteria [*sic*] as the indeterminacy or complementarity principles. Only if it acquires this *awareness of its own limits*, and avoids aspiring to an absolute form of knowledge, will one be able to consider semiotics as a *scientific* discipline [Eco, 1976, p. 129; emphasis in original].

Finally, any semiotic analysis will begin with an understanding of the interplay of *levels of analysis*, form and content, speech and language, formal rules and performances in a social setting. Take as an example a graduation ceremony, which would appear to be governed by formal rules, medieval traditions of dress, deference, and comportment, and past local traditions.

In a recent graduation in which I participated, the audience was allowed, and indeed encouraged, to yell out or cheer when the name of a family member was announced, to stand, take pictures, leave their seats, and otherwise become an active part of the ceremony, not a passive audience. Graduates appeared in robes, one carried a tiny baby dressed in a miniature cap and gown in front of her, all kissed and hugged various functionaries in the hooding ceremony, and people variously kissed, hugged, or shook hands with the dean of the school. The faculty did not know which side of the cap to place the tassel, did not know when to rise or remain seated (some took off their caps, others left them on), and did not know how to proceed in and out of their chairs on the stage. Some members of the class gave awards, and were not introduced. They had to walk on stage and announce themselves: "Hi!! I'm Suzy Schmaltz I don't know . . . I guess I'll just name the people we like . . . ." Some people walked across the stage, some strolled, and one Black woman raised her fist and led a small cheer after she was given her hood. Various levels of applause were given to people who crossed the stage (the least adequate students, those at the bottom of the class, recieved the largest and longest applause from their classmates, presumably because their finishing was remarkable). The faculty, when leaving, walked at uneven speeds, not together, unsure whether to walk with a partner, or in a line, and the audience arose and some left prior to the faculty recessional. Here, one can see the formal rules of dress, of order, of ceremony, interplaying with actual performance, as well as see individualistic variations on the role of student, faculty, and audience.

The analytic focus of semiotics is upon the graduation as a formal *ceremony*, for example, the order of events, the contrasting dress, the code of space (audience, faculty, graduating seniors), the signs of rank and status (caps, hoods of different colors, gowns and of varying styles and lengths), the conventions of address (rhetorical forms such as the welcoming address, the prayer, the main address, the students' thanks, and so on), the order of march and texts (such as programs, instructions to participants, and diplomas). Such forms can be analyzed in relation to performance, a suggestion of which is included in my description of the graduation, or could be looked at behaviorally or psychologically in terms of attitudes, personality systems, drives, or learning theory. The choice of a semiotic perspective does not obviate other sorts of data, or the interplay of form and content, or performance and structure.

The following section on semiotics builds on this orientation section. We discuss first the primary concepts of semiotics code: unit, metonym, metaphor, syntagm, paradigm, connotative and denotative meaning, semiosis, the interpretant, structuralism, context, and text. Some of the material is drawn from a study of police calls, which is discussed in detail in Chapter 3.

## Semiotics: The Science of Signs

Social life is a field of signs organized by other signs about signs that communicate various social relations. Sociology can be seen as a subfield of semiotics. Let us further explore this view.

Signs are composed of two inseparable entities, a *signifier* or *expression* that carries a message, and a *signified* or *content* that is conveyed. The connection that exists between the expression and the content is variable, and must be understood within a given set of rules or principles that guide the connections made. Connections, when identified, isolated, and formalized, can be assembled into a code. *Codes* themselves vary: Some codes are formal and logical, and the conventions or connections between expression and content quite specific and arbitrary (e.g., chemical formulae, computer programs), while other conventions are quite "natural" or commonsensical, such as the understanding that smoke and fire are correlated or that footprints on the sand indicate human presence. The consequences of coding are the focus of classic works of rhetoric, in which the intention was to uncover how certain social forms of communication produce a given meaning. The forms of these connections are various, such as opposition, metaphor (groupings by association or similarity), and metonymy (groupings by proximity, such as a string of names), and they are indicated or marked, as it were, in given domains in which clusters of meaning reside. For example, in sociology, some of them are roles, types of strategies, groups, and organizations.

Social practices, indicated by signs, are like language bits (morphemes, sememes; Eco, 1979b, ch. 2), connected as they are and subject, therefore, to the same kinds of analytic techniques. The aim of semiotic analysis is not mere description, but rather to uncover or discover the systems that the parts constitute and to "determine the nature of the system underlying the event" (Culler, 1975, p. 31). The purpose is to identify the elements of a system, and the system of which they are parts, in order to produce explanations of those constraints in formal and differentiated terms.

The meanings of importance in social life are *contextual* or domain-specific such that the relationship between the expression *plant* and the content "an industrial firm," "an organic living thing," and "placing something in the earth" (an example drawn from Minsky, 1968) is understood or implicit given a context or set of social relations. Thus one expression can, given a context, denote several contents, and, conversely, a single content may be referenced by several expressions. Most connections are made almost without knowing, based upon what is assumed or taken for granted. When farmers discuss "plants," or when business people negotiate over "plants," the expected links are understood. The marking of context is often implicit, but can be explicit, as when people ask, "Are we discussing the same sort of 'plants' here?" Formal organizations mark discourse in myriad ways to reduce the equivocality of messages, and to key a context.

Signs are presented in an order of some kind, and marking the syntactical and rule-bound aspects of this order as well as the semantic features is social and symbolic. Social life is, in fact, suffused with signs that communicate at several levels, either sequentially or metaphorically. A given set of signs made sensible by one code can be subsumed at another level by another code. The first set of connections, for example, "running shoes" as an *expression* and "Adidas" as content, are synecdochically connected at one level, while at the second level, the expression "sport" is linked to various forms of running (marathon, jogging, "10 K" runs). The connections of the first denotative relationship suggest a set of social roles in the context of running. At a third level of connotation, "play" can be linked metaphorically, through clothing, with leisure. From this chain of signification, one can see how social organization is signaled by a few cues given by a person. These cues can read off in ways that spiral "upward" to communicate "leisure" wear for some observers, and to communicate marathon runner (i.e., serious competitive sport) for others, or, of course, both at the same time. The first set of relationships perceived could be called *meaning*, but the sequence of signs about signs communicates the many faces of social order.

By attending to the codes (ways that content and expression are connected) that order given domains within social groups, and the meanings and social and behavioral responses that are associated with such coding, a conceptual apparatus for the analysis of culture is created. This lens permits isolating, characterizing, manipulating, and recombining elements of a cultural code in a systematic and formal fashion. This would appear to be an aim consistent with the avowed intentions of the family of sociologies, such as symbolic interactionism, phenemenological-existentialism, and ethnomethodology (excluding conversational analysis and its variants), to explicate social meanings. Barley makes a rather useful summary statement (1983, p. 398):

A semiotic approach to the study of culture elevates the presumption of a socially shared system of meanings from the status of a background assumption to the explicit focus of investigation and implies that behavioral regularity is a necessary, but not sufficient, condition for the explication of cultural understanding.

Semiotics, as a culturally based discipline, makes a number of assumptions about social life in addition to the fundamental idea that we inhabit a world of overlapping systems of signs, signs about signs, and metacoding of such systems in such units as "nation-states," "cultures," and even "organizations." Semiotics assumes that language is the model for other sorts of social relations.

Semiotics, the science of signs, is a basis for structuralism, or the study of wholes as constituted by elements that form them (see Kurzweil, 1980; Robey, 1973; Pettit, 1977; Hawkes, 1977). The degree to which analysis seeks fully formalized, quasi-algebraic formulations, pattern, and tautology discriminates among those who advocate some version of structuralism. Critics have suggested that the absence of a body of detailed research, based on closely gathered and refined data drawn from a given domain of social life, makes it difficult to assess claims made for possessing general explanations of the functioning of sign systems. Perhaps most important, the implication of such criticism is that the static and abstract concern with rules, codes, formal oppositions, and systems of kinship, colors, or myths simply substitutes formalism for functionalism of various kinds. Unless it is possible to show how semiotic analyses can produce an account of the results of the production of sign systems, they can be dismissed as iconic cartoons of what has been regarded as proper sociological analyses.

## CHANGE IN STRUCTURALISM

A common criticism of the various forms of structuralism is that they do not provide explanations for change. (Of course, this criticism is rather easily directed to most social science perspectives.) *Structuralist theories* are glossed here as those that (a) contain a focus upon binary oppositions within linguistic systems, (b) utilize the model of language as a fundamental metaphor for explaining (some) social relations, (c) view discourse as the primary focus of analysis, and (d) attempt to explain the production of discourse and texts with relatively formal rules and principles (see Lemert, 1979b). The variations around these themes are many and varied, and explication of their relative strengths and weaknesses should be sought elsewhere (Kurzweil, 1980; Sturrock, 1979). Within these theories, there are quite different emphases on "change."

Two approaches to change attempt to explain alteration of a given structure. The classic position of de Saussure was that since the idea of "system" itself was always a notional one, the dynamic between the posited formal characteristics of the system and the practice of speaking, that is, a relative and relational matter, required a focus on both sychronic (single time) and diachronic (a system studied in time) matters. Later developments and criticisms of de Saussure, as adopted by Lévi-Strauss, made much of the notion of *différence* in meaning as a value question (punning on the term *déférence* in French) (see Derrida, 1976), and claimed that previous structural analysis had frozen signifiers to single meanings and contexts. The varied and competing codes and semantic fields within any text were identified by Derrida and others, and the dialectics within language systems and the poetic nature of the meanings were elevated. The mathematically based notion of transformations and the preeminence of any given mode of communication were challenged.

A rather different analytic focus is the application of structuralism to the analysis of process. The key question is how the *interpretant* is to be understood. The interpretant is that which guarantees the validity of the sign regardless of the interpreter (Eco, 1979b, p. 68). Eco asserts, in a view adopted here as well, that the interpretant is "another representation which is referred to the same object." Consider several examples of interpretants. I examine the program for an East Lansing High School soccer game. The context is thus that of games with programs listing names and numbers. I can connect the *expression* "all" with the implicit (not listed on this program) "position played" (the backs are lowest, the halfbacks slightly higher, and the offensive forwards are higher still). Knowledge of positions is the interpretant here. Note that the relationship is symmetrical so that one can read the position on the field as an indication of possible number a person might have as well as use the number to determine the position. Such conventions are also used in American football with number descending from ends, tackles, guards, and centers to the backfield. I can read the *expression* "personal name" (especially last name) as a key to another *content*, "kinship relations" between the player and his sister(s), brother(s), mother, or father. In this case, I draw on my knowledge of East Lansing families, and the acquaintances of my three children who are recent graduates. The interpretant here is my knowledge of family names. I can also link the presence or absence of a number (expression) as a key to the "position played" (content), since goalkeepers wear bright single-color uniforms without numbers. My knowledge there is twice-determined in that I can see the goalkeeper in the net and know that that is his position as well as knowing that a player without a number and in plain uniform is a goalkeeper. In other words, the physical place of the goalkeeper on the field refers to his position, whereas the position of other players on the field is only indicative of their role or position at the point of a kickoff to initiate play. Finally, the interpretant can be more personal. I might see the number 11 as my son's number when he played; I connect the *expression* "11" with the *content*, "Sean Peter Manning." This may be done also by others, but it would be a connection that few would share without explanations.

The advantage of social conventions guiding expression and content is that they are assumed and institutionalized connections that one shares with a large number of people; they are a constitutive feature of the game soccer and of other games. Eco points out that this view demands that there be an unlimited process of interpretation in semiotics, insofar as to discover what the interpretant of a sign is (to establish its validity, or the source of its meaning), it is necessary to name it by means of another sign, and so on. A definition of a sign in this context is derived from Peirce, who claims that a sign is incomplete; it is anything that determines something else to refer to an object to which it itself refers (its object) in the same way, the interpretant becoming in turn a sign, and so on ad infinitum (Peirce, 1931-1958, quoted by Eco, 1979b, p. 69). The constant reference "forward and back," as it were, is semiosis, or the process by which empirical subjects communicate, communicaiton processes being made possible by the organization of the signification system (Eco, 1979b, p. 316). Each signifier is given meaning by its signified, which in turn signifies another signified, and so on. The interpretation of such relationships within an organizational context must encompass the serial consequences that the interpretants elicit. Chains of signification contain time in their linear unfolding quality. Alteration in the levels of signification produce differentiation. It is possible to demonstrate, for example, that certain sorts of chains are reproduced in various sociotechnical systems (social roles emerging from the relationships between workers and technology). This illustrates structural replication, or the reproduction of structure in social systems. Conversely, if chains of signification differ in different subsystems of a system or organization, then a source of tension is identified that may cause changes within an organizational code. This last conception of change is built upon several points that require underscoring.

The concern is with codes and their interrelationships, not the referential function of language. Any attempt to find a concrete referent for a sign will simply produce another sign, itself only defined by means of cultural conventions (see Eco, 1979b, p. 68). These searches commit the fallacy of seeking the metaphysical present, and they deny the symbolic and cultural web within which social relations are transacted. In other words, the referent is not a discriminate parameter among signs. Only their relations to each other are considered. The ideational nature of semiotics is such that even ideas are viewed as signs of a sort (Eco, 1979b, pp. 165-167). *Encoding*, or the process of subsuming phenomena to a code, is seen as both decoding and encoding simultaneously (since any sign that can be considered as such is coded in some fashion, any action of encoding involves extracting it from one code and entering it into another). Encoding is possible because codes can be combined, conflated, reversed, and layered together, that is, expression and content in one can become a sign in a secondary coding system, and so on.

The transfer of signs across codes can occur within a given social system or subsystem. The differentiation and integration of signs can be seen within a single subsystem, synchronically, as it were, as well as across subsystems of social roles diachronically.

The transfer process, in turn—seen concretely as the movement of messages through boundaries—produces a series of consequences: (a) layered meanings, insofar as denotations and connotations pyramid upward, creating a kind of rainbow texture of meanings; (b) behavioral responses resulting from interpretations made of these chains of signification, and interpretation of these interpretations (especially as, for example, one takes one's cues about action from the interpretation made of the other person's interpretation of a set of signals); and (c) a field of potentially contradictory semantic fields that themselves are variously coherent and variously attached to authoritative sources of marking (power structures). The relationships obtaining among the codes in the field are shifting and not stable.

It should be stated clearly that all such analyses are themselves made possible by a theory of communication that includes as a "hidden operator" in sign systems: the human actor with an attitude toward communication. The actor provides the interpretant. The relevance of this view, which contrasts with some versions of semiology, will become increasingly clear.

Much fieldwork involves the interpretation of texts, many of which are gathered within an organization, group, or from a historical period. The concept of *text* as a set of interlocking signs understood by the application of several codes is central to both data-gathering and analysis (see Eco, 1984, chs. 5, 6.).

## TEXTS AND CONTEXTS

Although the notion of *social context* has great appeal and is related to a family of concepts with enduring explanatory power, such as thick description (Geertz, 1973), group and grid (Douglas, 1970), elaborated and restricted codes (Bernstein, 1971), and field, tenor, and code (Halliday, 1978), it remains a rather vague and mercurial concept. Context would appear to reference aspects of the social-psychological world of the speaker and the hearer that, in addition to a message, are necessary features of meaningful communications (see Ochs, 1979, cited in Levinson, 1983, p. 23). Conversational analysis, which has been most specifically concerned to specify the work of context in producing meaningful talk, relies on rather implicit notions, although the work of Sacks includes attention to setting specific-meanings or categorizations (Garfinkel and Sacks, 1970).

The role of context is obviously crucial in organized settings that daily process a large number of telephone calls from the public. Calls that may be as brief as 30 seconds provide a bare minimum of information, and yet require rapid decisions involving allocation of personnel, equipment, and resources to a reported trouble. Because in police, fire, and emergency services, telephone calls that omit nonverbal signs normally accompanying speech are the primary means of communication, commonsense knowledge of behavior, along with organization-specific occupational and organizational culture (Barley, 1983) are used to fill in, construct, and infer meanings. These calls and their interpretation are context-dependent communication, and their analysis should permit a further explication of the relevance of context to organizational communications.

Organizations are formally constituted systems for the processing of communicational units utilizing set technology, a structure of roles and tasks, systems of encoding and decoding meaning, and interpretative practices (see Manning, 1982a, 1985b, in press). From the diversity of messages produced by the public, they must introduce routine, regularity, consistency; they must readily convert equivocal and uncertain messages (nature) into organizationally actionable work (culture).

Communicational units, such as messages, records, memos, and *aides-memoire*, are sanctioned within an organization, normalized, and marked to minimize equivocation, noise, and ambiguity. As such, they are selectively assembled sets of signs or information formed to introduce variation that is manageable as well as to ensure relatively nonproblematic processing of such units. Written records are texts that have an organizational reality stabilized by recursive processing within a communicational system. The process of converting everyday language as transformed into organizational texts is a matter of seeing these messages as having components, encoding these components into the system of classification of the organization, transmitting the messages through the organization, and producing action outcomes.

The written texts that are assembled, such as a call about a burglary, may contain several messages and, depending on how they are interpreted, communicate at several levels. Thus a burglary of an old and blind woman given a number and priority (denoted) may be viewed as a crime, seen as morally disgusting, granted a degree of occupational importance as "good police work," and understood as an unfolding story (connoted) (see Eco, 1979b, p. 6).

The texts that are produced thus communicate denotatively and connotatively, at several levels of meaning, and can be seen as stories or narratives about social life brought to police attention. Through this transformation activity, everyday tales and troubles are returned to the speaker like an echo in which words once previously said are now reheard with new pitch, speed, frequency, and volume and seemingly emitted from a different source.

The notion of organization text that is critical here assumes that readers provide an interpretative frame for their reading that draws on culturally accepted modes of interpretative (codes), conventions about how and what to read from and into any communication or text, and connections that are drawn between the units of the communication and an ongoing sequence of actions or functions (see Barthes, 1975; Culler, 1975). The social role of the reader, the associative contexts utilized to cluster and connect as well as differentiate the relevant signs within the text, the conventions about what constitutes a communicational unit, and the technology in which the message is sent and received, all shape a text.

Rules about how one does this, or metacommunicative rules (Bateson, 1972, p. 179; Eco, 1979, p. 154), are related to but cannot be derived from formal organization procedures, organizational charts of authority, occupational cultures, or the law (see Jackson, 1985; Cicourel, 1984). When messages move through subsystems of organiza-

42

tions, each with ways of adding connotative or "mythological" (Barthes, 1972) levels of meaning, they acquire an *intertextuality* or reflexivity. They refer to other texts within themselves (Kristeva, 1981, p. 15). The concept of a message is a function of a cognitively or semantically isolated text within an organizational field.

Classic textual analysis derived from formalists (Propp, Shklovski, and Jakobson summarized, by Todorov, 1981) identifies three aspects of texts: the *semantic*, or the meaning of texts, the mode of presentation, or *style* of messages, and the *syntactical*, or the structure of texts. It is the latter that is of concern here. Structural analysis of texts examines the functional relationship between units of the text, narrative, or story, and the modes of combination of the units (their spatial and temporal ordering). Once the units and the objects are identified, one has a unit-system of acts and consequences, the model of which is the sentence with subject, object, and verb (Fowler, 1977). The combinations and sequences by which units are orchestrated into narrative ideally require that an entire text be analyzed. However, in organizational analysis, the dictionary of available meanings, the formats and classification system, the resources of natural language (grammar and syntax), as well as roles, interpretation, and technology form an underlying machinery for the production of texts (see Woolgar and Latour, 1979; Knorr-Cetina, 1981). The plots, figures, and spatial-temporal relations as well as the perspective or modality (the voice of the text—who speaks?) are organizationally constrained. Given a text, assumptions are made about underlying rules that may order both their production and their contents.

## Summary

These concepts are meant as tools for the analysis of everyday life. They are keys to cultural competence. They have a generality that permits one to look at the principles that make meaningful communication as found in formal or informal sign systems, those that are open or closed, written or verbal, and to look at the origins of meaning in conventions, in connotative and denotative meanings, and at stasis as well as change. Clearly, the more formal, closed, written, denotative, and rule-based the system, such as Morse code, mathematics, logic, or rules governing parking on university parking lots, the more accessible are the surface meanings. The more subtle and difficult issues of American social life, such as the negotiation of conversations, "good manners," and even rules governing formal ceremonies are so variegated, situational, and regionally based, that enormous commonsense understanding must underlie and precede any formal analysis. Hence, one can see *the essential role of fieldwork in connection with formal semiotic analysis.*

The following chapter presents some examples of fieldwork using semiotics. Some of the problems that are involved in moving from concrete data about a setting or organization and semiotic analysis are identified.

## 3. SEMIOTICS AND FIELDWORK: SOME EXAMPLES

The orientation of semiotics moves it toward formalization. This entails specifying given units of analysis within a context, searching for principles, rules or oppositions, and manifesting an explicit comparative focus. Semiotics is a complement to the descriptive and case-based orientation of most fieldwork. The issues that semiotics in fieldwork highlight result from acceptance of the orientation. Here, we outline some attempts to explore the consequences of fieldwork based upon the semiotic method.

### Semiotic Principles

It should be emphasized that semiotics is an analytic technique, not a data-gathering technique. Most fieldwork, and much of the fieldwork literature, focuses on data-gathering. Semiotics can serve functions that the following examples should serve to clarify.

Semiotics is a mode of *problem identification.* Thus, for example, in my work on police communication (in press), I was interested in the problem of the orientation of the communication following a semiotic model introduced by Jakobson (1960).

A series of problems result from using this model of the communication system. First, how are the participants *oriented* to the messages? Second, what are the possible *channels* of communication within the various segments of the police organization? Third, what are the *effects* of each of the orientations on the communicational system? If speakers are oriented, for example, to the informational aspects of the message, what aspects of human communication (affective symbolism, contact among people, shared values) are depressed in salience? Fourth, what are the *metalinguistic* (social) aspects of the communication that operate in an organization to allow people to know what code is being used and shared? This is particularly important in police-public communications where some shared understanding is *essential* to providing the service.

Semiotics is a mode of pursuing the relevant *units of analysis* within a context. These are analytic terms, some derived from linguistics, others from sociology. In my work on English policing (1977, 1979), I was interested in units used to partition relations with the public and within the force. I found that there was a *social code* for giftlike transactions. It began on one end with gift, then perk, then mump, then skiving, corruption, and crime. At one end, a *gift* was freely given with no reciprocity expected on either side; such matters might include drinks from publicans, gifts at holidays from the public, reduction in the costs of goods and services at shops, and so on. A *perk* was an earned gift in the context on the job, and so involved some kind of reciprocity among colleagues. A *mump* was a gift that was not (likely) to be reciprocated, and was unearned, such as begging a cigarette or small change from someone. A *skiv* was an unearned gift within the job such as avoiding duties, slacking off in expected effort, or failing to carry out a task on time. *Corruption* was an unearned gain that may have involved failure to carry out duties. Finally, *crime* for these police was unthinkable, but a logical end of the continuum. They claimed it did not happen; that no officer they knew had committed a crime. Crime was self-serving and unearned, illegal, and damaging to others. In this little example from my fieldwork among the London Metropolitan police, a taxonomy of items is created within the context of exchange and each unit contrasts with the other. From these units in context, one can move to connections between these actions and others such as high-speed chases, corruption investigation, and problems of command in the occupational culture (Manning, 1979, 1980, 1982b).

Semiotics is a way of *formalizing analysis*. In the following sections, it will be seen that in the units in the communicational system itself, one can find the paradigms or associational contexts within which the *syntagms* (units in a message in this case) are understood. One can then compare these across the organization as messages move from one segment of the police (operators, dispatchers, officers on patrol), between organizations (my analysis reports studies of two police departments, one in America and one in Britain), and at different levels of communication. One can also produce rules and generalizations about how, for example, messages are heard. Such rules as "use the bare minimum possible bits of information to characterize a message"; or "assume that people are talking about events occurring now (in 'real time')," rather than, on one hand, in dreams or fantasies, or, on the other, in past events. These are, in effect, the *constitutive conventions* (Culler, 1975, p. 30) that allow sets of signs to be heard within a police code and, therefore, to have reproducible and valid meaning within the police system. One meaning can rest upon another. For example, when a video of Huey Lewis and the News singing "The Heart of Rock and Roll [is still beating]" shows old rock stars performing, it's suggesting or connoting connection over time between rock music and rock musicians. On one level of meaning, the heart of rock and roll is beating now, but it has also beat in the past. Historical continuity is communicated at another level. The heartbeat sound that thumps at the beginning and end of the record is synecdochical (it is a part representing the whole), representing the whole body of music on one hand and people who listen on the other (they are the heart in a metaphoric sense). Huey Lewis himself is but one part of the whole, the body of rock and roll, and, in that sense, represents the heart. He is the foreground against which in the background performers such as Bill Haley ("Rock around the Clock," the first very popular rock and roll hit song), various English groups, and Elvis Presley appear, sing, and dance. This is an iconic (pictorial) representation of the place of Huey Lewis in a series (metonymical ordering by proximity) of people, with all of whom he shares musical taste. This is also a rendering of two themes, "Rock and roll never dies," because the heartbeat begins at the record and ends it, fading in and fading out (but still beating), as well as "Rock and Roll never forgets," because in the background are all the progenitors of the genre playing and singing today as always. The existence of a number of other themes, for example, "rock and roll is human" (it has heart in the cliché sense of producing warm feelings), "this rock and roll is alive," whereas other past artists and styles are dead, and the superordinate status of Huey Lewis and the News over other bands suggests that while these symbols denote several meanings, they also have a number of broader connotative meanings. The decision to stop after two or three levels or themes, to establish relative importance of one theme over another, to resolve contradictory or ambiguous symbols or clusters of symbols are aesthetic matters. A convincing case must be made. Unlike most sociology, but like qualitative sociology generally, this analysis does not rely on frequency distributions, correlations among variables, or other forms of statistical inference.

Semiotics permits, indeed, requires *comparisons*. Semiotics is based on the central notions of opposition in context as the source of meaning (whether this is linked to an assumption about the nature of human cognition or binary oppositions is arguable and unnecessary for the argument made here (see Leach, 1976). This means that studies of single cases, or types, or groups, must involve implicit but perhaps unrecognized comparisons. Thus explicit comparison is urged. Studying two police communications systems (Manning, in press), it was found that the *format* within which messages were cast (in part determined by the computer engineers who established the command and control system), the *ecology* of the two organizations (how the messages passed from one part of the organization to the other), the *roles and tasks* assigned to officers, and the *interpretations* that were made of the messages differed in the two organizations. Thus the general comparative model of semiotics not only requires comparison to establish meaning, but patterns research to include more than one social group, organization, occupation, class, neighborhood, or the like.

Semiotics requires that analysis *penetrate surface* meanings or mere description and extract underlying modes of understanding. For example, it might be assumed that the meaning of any given message, glossed by a single term such as *burglary*, *robbery*, or *rape*, would be constant across segments of police organizations, would be stable in organizations, if compared, and would be denotatively precise since it would be assumed to be the basis on which police were dispatched to assist people. These are all given in single surface meaning, or the denotative gloss on a citizen's message such as "I've been raped at my apartment, 2900 Northwind, number 717." Data reported below indicated that none of these assumptions is true. If one adopts a semiotic model of analysis, one finds that different meanings are attached in different segments, that there are a number of associated meanings or connotative meanings associated with such crime categories, and that different police organizations understand them to mean different things. This understanding of police communication results from looking at *semiosis*, or changes in meaning over time.

Semiotics assumes *different perspectives* on social life. In the analysis of the perspective of the operators, dispatchers, and officers on the message glossed with the term *rape* (below), it is assumed that different connotative meanings are implicit, or unstated, in the communications between segments. The analysis of the perspectival shift required of controllers (below) involves reconstructing the controller's thinking about the event that is being called about by the public, the view of the operator who took the message to send on to the controller, and the officer to whom the controller must send the message. The controller is taking the roles of the other and the perspective of the other, as well as integrating them into his own understanding of what is required of him (all controllers are men in this department). The question then arises: How do they understand each other sufficiently to organize and mobilize collective action to achieve an end? This question is in part answered by looking at the shared occupational culture that each officer assumes that others share with him or her. This provides broader principles, working rules, and rules of thumb seen as shared (Manning, 1982a).

The purpose of enumerating these broad points about semiotics is that they distinguish semiotics from other modes of sociological work, at least in combination, although several of them are characteristic of other approaches such as symbolic interactionism. It also will serve to sensitize the reader to ways of thinking about semiotic fieldwork and set the stage for thinking about the more detailed examples that follow. In the examples, the attempt will be made to illustrate some of the key issues within semiotics to which my fieldwork is addressed. They are given in order of generality, and are not exclusive of other issues a semiotician might examine.

As was mentioned above, one of the key issues in semiotics, or in any formal approach to social life, is conceptualization of change. In the work presented below on message movements in two police departments, the idea of semiosis, or the change in meaning as the change in the interpretant (that which is the fixed point that gives connection between *expression* and *content*) is presented. Thus change in meaning is addressed by looking at aspects of the context that fix meaning, or things other than the expression and content itself that clarify the meaning of messages.

This meaning may take conventional forms. Semiotics studies language in relation to social life, and in forms of language expression such as stories, folklore, speeches, myths, novels, poems, and discourse itself. The analysis of messages as a social form thus contributes to the study of discourse and of narratives themselves. Are calls to the police like folktales? Discourse involves not only forms of narrative, but patterns of association and dissociation.

What are some of the metaphors of social life? How do these work in organizations? How does one think about one thing in terms of another, and what are the consequences? What are the metaphors of policing, of nuclear safety, or organizations more generally?

In organizations, what are the units, the syntagms and paradigms, most central in official modes of communication? What are the units of a message, and how are messages seen as like each other or different, or clustered into groups? Do these differ by perspective or unit of an organization?

How does one identify different perspectives on a concept or expressions such as *safety*, *policy*, or *nuclear reactor*? Let us consider some examples.

## Semiotic Fieldwork

### POLICY

The example describes the formal features of the concept "policy" as it is used within the British Nuclear Installations Inspectorate (NII).[1] The Nuclear Installations Inspectorate functions with the Health and Safety Executive and was first established in 1969. It came under the Health and Safety Executive with the Act of 1973. It is composed of five branches: future reactors, policy, current reactors, reactors under construction, and fuel reprocessing, each headed by a principal inspector and including approximately 20 people each (there are many fewer in the policy branch, and slightly more than 20 in each of the other four). They have a mandate to ensure that safety is maintained by the industry, and that the safety of workers and the surrounding community is considered in planning, siting, and operations. They carry out their duties by consultation on design, construction, maintenance, siting, and safety features, management of the reactor, as well as through inspection, research (a very minor role, although some research is done on their behalf by consultants), and audits. The largest number of inspectors are trained in the sciences, engineering, and/or have experience in the industry itself. All but one of the 105 inspectors are men. Examples are drawn from interviews and case analysis. Once these formal features are set out (some 11 have been identified), they will be sorted into *cognitive clusters*, or ways of thinking about policy-problems. These cognitive clusters, or metaphors, can be integrated at additional levels so that broad conceptions of the nature of the organization and its mandate can be identified. Once these analyses have been outlined, some of the tensions and difficulties that arise within NII as a result of different meanings of policy are discussed.

This preliminary analysis of meanings is based upon a cognitive mapping procedure, the aim of which is to map the organization's view of the world and its view of its relationship to that world-map. It can be used to read off readings of the social and technical world of concern to NII, as well as the different readings that are possible, given one's view of policy. It indicates the location of authority for policymaking within the organization, and identifies the differing conceptions of the causes, locations, and solutions to safety problems. It is limited because it is a formulation based on a verbal or cognitive construction of the social world and does not include behaviors, feelings, and tacit knowledge.

In Figure 3.1, one can see 11 *competing meanings* associated with the term *policy* (column A). It should also be noted that the method of eliciting the points was to ask in open-ended questions what interviewers' notions of policy were. From these replies, I drew out repeated themes, grouping and collapsing some, giving the groups names, and trying to order them. This is something like the process of creating a code for entering raw data, and is partially guided by conceptual ideas from fields such as organizational theory. Column A lists denotative (specific) meanings of the term *policy*. As one moves from left to right, the meanings are broader, more complex semantically, and perhaps in conflict with the earlier deconstructed meanings. At the next level of analysis, one can cluster these into slightly broader groupings of connotative meanings (column B). These are *metaphors* of policy. Metaphors or paradigms are contexts of association of meaning; the lines in Figure 3.1 indicate denotative meanings that can be regrouped to show similarities among them. Metaphors are clusters of definitions of policy; they are located within institutions (NII). If these six metaphors are grouped into broader institutional concerns (column C), four are identified: temporal process, functional roles, emergent structure, and

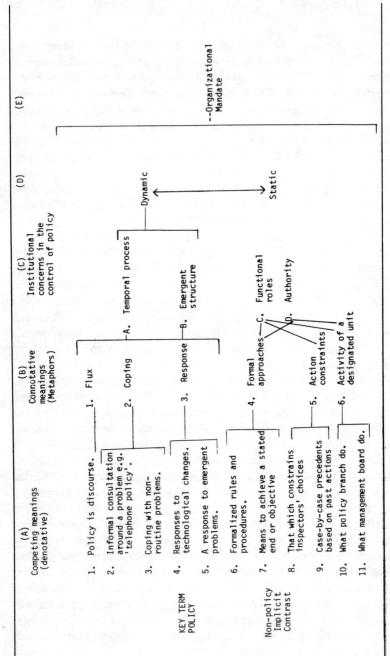

Figure 3.1. A Semiotic of Policy.

authority. These are organizing perspectives on problems to which the idea of policy is brought. Institutional concerns are foci of political and organizational action; the ways in which the organization sees its own action, how it imagines others see it, and how it wishes to represent itself. In some broad fashion (column D), there is an oppositional dynamic, doing and action, and static, obligation and responsibility. That is, policy is seen as something one does or something one has a duty to perform as a reflective and self-conscious matter. Dynamic/static is an *opposition* between very broad beliefs held about policy. All the meanings of policy (columns A through D) are integrated by belief in the organization as a whole seen as its mandate.

*Mandate* is the organization's view of its legal and moral domain of authoritative action as defined by the public (see Hughes, 1970).

The relevance of these points to a working definition of *policy* is that if one views the social and technical world as a flux, for example, then this is reflected in the discourse about policy in that world. If the technical world is seen as running ahead of the capacity to anticipate it fully, then notions of coping and response will dominate policy ideas. These are examples of the connection between the social and technical world and policy. Conceptions of cause and blame are also related insofar as if one can anticipate and control, one has a conception of policy as more static perhaps than if one's conception of problems is that they are emergent. The conception of institutional responsibility and authority is noted in the figure when named locations, functions, or structures are seen as policy loci, but it is also implicit in column C, which suggests points at which focal action will be taken within the organization to control, shape, intervene, or anticipate the nature of policy by management. There may not be agreement among the various levels within the inspectorate about what should actually be done about the problem or the policy seen as relevant to that problem.

In brief summary, this outline does not describe what is actually done about problems; this is the structure by which problems are constituted. These differences, further, are not necessarily divisive because general beliefs, management, and supervision, division of labor into branches with specified duties and horizons of concern, and levels of organization mitigate and blur these different cognitive maps. As a result, these views are not equally valid or legitimated within the organization; some are more equal than others as modes of policy analysis, and, indeed, some are empirically more widely espoused than others. Finally, these developments mean change in the direction of formal, written, and centralized notions of policy.

## THE POLICE ORGANIZATIONS

The two organizations studied were one in the United Kingdom, called the British Police Department (BPD), and one in the United States, called the Midwest Police Department (MPD). The studies from which the data were gathered are varied. The focus of this project was to determine through observation and interpretation how the messages were defined; what the organizations were viewed as doing with and to such messages; and how codes into which the messages were placed, the social organization of the various subsystems, and the technology employed affected the interpretation of the messages received. Patterns of similarity and difference between and among the organizations and the organizational subsystems were sought. There were several overtly similar characteristics of the two organizations and areas (the sizes of the cities and of the forces, centralized computerized systems of call processing and computer-assisted dispatching, and, to a lesser degree, the social composition of the areas). The two organizations were located in large industrialized cities over 2.7 million inhabitants, and employed over 5000 sworn officers.

The focus of this research is the police communication system itself, as embedded in the larger structure of policing. Each police organization takes calls in a centralized computer center (999 calls in Britain, 911 in the United States), sorts out calls, determines the service required, and assigns or refers the call. The focus is, in many respects, upon the coding system itself, its operation, and the movement and interpretation of messages as they flow through the Police Communication System (PCS). In the BPD, the department from which these examples are drawn, phone messages are received by operators in a large center from 999 and other lines. They are then entered into microcomputers using a set format and sent to the police subdivisions in the city. The police officers with the rank of sergeant who receive the calls on the screen, take radio messages, and process calls coming directly to that subdivision, are called *controllers*. Although the center can bypass the subdivision and send a message directly to a dog squad or other specialized forcewide group, most calls are sent by computer to appear on the visual display unit (VDU) and are received by the controller. The message can be sent direct, via VHF (long distance command for fast response cars and dog-units) or UHF (subdivisional) radio and teleprinter (which eventually prints out the messages sent between the center and the controllers), or the PNC (Police National Computer). The message format includes date, time, incident number, classification, assignment, location, caller's name, message results, and other details of the decisions made by officers with respect to the incident. (The BPD's message format is much more detailed in this respect than that of the MPD). When the controller receives the message, he or she can reclassify it; refuse to act; put it in the queue for further action; decide that it does not require police attention; treat it as a message or information; or assign it, either by phone, by radio (UHF), or directly verbally to someone in the room. Calls are also received by the controller via the subdivisional phone, or as relayed from clerks in the reserve room, and these can be assigned or dealt with informally. All messages that arrive via the VDU are held in the machine until reported as finished or closed by the controller. In effect, he or she has a record of all in-progress incidents, and is responsible for monitoring police and other actions and for entering the disposition of the incident. Other work done on the subdivision does not require this record, so that work load figures—numbers of calls and incidents handled officially—do not in fact represent the total number of jobs done, work assigned, or even the number of calls to the police. Data from the formal assignments are entered in the computer at the end of each day, printed out, and sent to each subdivision. Organizations provide preestablished means for making sense of any call. The police, for example, have a set *format* (callers' name, address, and phone number, nature of the problem, and so on) that contains units or *syntagms* and formalized categories in a classificatory system. This structure contains an implicit view of the world that converts the public's everyday language and experience into police-relevant communications. It is a formal grid, or signs about signs, which requires, nevertheless, interpretive work so that any call made to a police operator can be put into the format, placed into a category, and once so classified, grouped with other messages both as one in a series and as a type or sort of call. An example may show how these formal and "informal" or cognitive matters are related in the processing of police messages. It should be emphasized at this point that the assumption of this analysis is that the syntagms discovered are not exhaustive of those used to convey meaning in this department. Further, it does not explore, except by implication, how the informal meanings discussed below can contradict the formal meanings conveyed by the syntagms and paradigms identified. It is this kind of contradiction and its resolution that fieldwork is best suited to explore.

A caller rings the police, reports "my house has been broken into," and gives a name and address. The call is framed as a message and typed onto a VDU according to a set format in a given order. The key item in the format (1 of some 11 syntagms in the organization studied) is the category it is given by the operator. There are 30 categories (see Figure 3.2) used by the police studied (and the call can be double-categorized and/or recategorized). This is the basis for further assignments by police controllers who are sent the message from the operators. This call will be given an "11": burglary house/dwelling. The connection between the classification system and the encodation done by a given operator, for example, how this operator decides the call is about a burglary is informal and tacit, but there is a systematic relationship between the units and the classificatory system or code (see Manning, 1985b). The work of establishing connections, or hearing "11" as burglary or "06" as assault, is done by implicit understandings or contrasts between the expressions (the categories) and the contents (the words) and differences between expressions and contents and other contents. "11" (a content) is linked to burglary (an expression); they denote each other. Established conventions within the police mean that one is heard and seen as the other.

As seen in Figure 3.3, the sign (burglary/11), a combination of expression and content, can act as an expression for yet another content, crime. Crime is more connotative meaning supplied by officers in the field, which can then become an expression for another content, possible arrest. Each of these linked sets, layered one upon the other, is part of a signifying chain. Seen as a whole, however, the message 11/burglary can be placed into a cognitive grouping of other similar calls or put within an associative context or paradigm. The *associative context* may have to do with the action requirements of the call, its potential for good police work, or what was done to dispose of it. The most obvious distinction or context is crime and noncrime calls, since the former are much sought and well regarded by officers.

Through this work of encoding, formatting, interpreting, and placing in context, police processing converts or transforms calls into jobs and produces a layering of meanings that moves a long way from the social

The list below can be obtained on screen by sending after entering the reporting officer's number [In a 'CHANGE FINAL CLASS' option in a recall the list can be displayed by entering a question mark (?) in the data field.]

| | | |
|---|---|---|
| 01. RTA INJURY | 11. BURGLARY D/HOUSE | 21. ILLNESS |
| 02. RTA NON INJURY | 12. BURGLARY OTHER | 22. INJURY |
| 03. ALARM ARREST | 13. DAMAGE CRIMINAL | 23. SUDDEN DEATH |
| 04. ALARM TO ARREST | 14. DAMAGE OTHER | 24. DRUNK |
| 05. ALARM FALSE | 15. THEFT OF CARS | 25. TRESPASS |
| 06. ASSAULTS | 16. THEFT FROM CARS | 26. ALCOTEST |
| 07. SEX OFFENCES | 17. OTHER THEFTS | 27. FALSE/MALICIOUS |
| 08. DISORDER | 18. OTHER CRIMES | 28. NO TRACE |
| 09. DOMESTIC DISPUTES | 19. VEHS OBST OR ABND | 29. MESSAGES |
| 10. MISSING PERSONS | 20. FIRES | 30. MISCELLANEOUS |

Up to three can be entered, each separated by a space. If a Change Final Class Option on recall is used, then new codes will overwrite the previous. If appropriate, therefore, reenter the previous code(s) with the new.

**Figure 3.2. The Final Classifications of Incidents and Resource Summary Codes, BPD.**

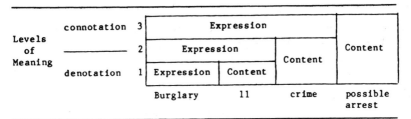

**Figure 3.3.** An Example of Denotative and Connotative Meanings of the Sign 11/Burglary in the BPD.

world of the person who makes the original call. It is precisely this process of text-message production that a semiotic analysis would permit one to explicate.

To summarize, the first example is one of *perspective*, and shows that a given term, *policy* (a signifier or an expression), is linked to quite different signifieds, or contents, depending on the context within which the work is used. The second example is a detailed study of the BPD that proceeds from finding *syntagms*, or units in the calls to the police, then identifies *paradigms*, or associative contexts and subcontexts. The third is a study of *narratives*, or stories, that are found in calls to the police. The aim here is to penetrate surface meanings to find unity in the structure of the narratives and in the types of stories processed in the BPD. The fourth is an analysis of change in meaning over time, or *semiosis*, and draws on data from the study of the MPD. The ordering of the following examples is based on the idea that first one searches for broad matters of context and organizational meanings, then one searches out the units of analysis, or the syntagms, and then searches for the contexts or paradigms that order them. Finally, the most difficult matters to establish in any fieldwork are questions of process, change, redefinition, and reorientation of groups to the fields of meaning within which they reside. These four examples, in turn, will assist us in the last chapter of the book in further integrating semiotics and fieldwork.

**SYNTAGMS AND PARADIGMS[2]**

*Syntagms.* If when presented with a communication, controllers in the BPD are oriented to the message (and not to the field, other activities in the setting, or noise) and to the units within the message rather than simply to passing on the message, they will logically or cognitively partition the incidents for assignment into 10 discernible units or syntagms. These are as follows (and are also shown in Table 3.1):

(1) time of receipt of the call by the operator before/during/after an event),
(2) source (public/alarm/police/direct line) of the original call,
(3) channel on which the incident is transmitted to the controller (radio/VDU/telephone/in person),
(4) location of the event (address/place/site/other),[3]
(5) caller's role (or the collar number of a police constable calling),
(6) caller's location (address/place/site/call box),
(7) persons acting to make the call (police/citizen/organization),
(8) reported actions of persons (police/citizens/agencies),
(9) direction of action reported in the incident, and
(10) descriptive term for the action reported in the incident.

The nine incidents listed below (all the calls received in one hour by a controller in one subdivision, here called "Queen's Fields") are analyzed. It should be noted that these syntagms are not taken exclusively from the format used to transmit the calls. Items 1, 2, 4, 6, and 10 are on the VDU transmission of the incident. The collar number of the PC calling will be included also (5). The remainder of the syntagms are inferred by the controllers from the message or, as in item 3, the channel on which it arrives is obvious to them. The subunits for each of these (in parentheses) are analytic distinctions derived from interviews with the controllers.

Table 3.1. Syntagms Found in Recorded Incidents from Nine Calls at Queens' Fields (January 1980)[a]

| Syntagm | 1 | 2 | 3 | 4 | 5 | 6 | 7 | 8 | 9 |
|---|---|---|---|---|---|---|---|---|---|
| | | | | | Call | | | | |
| 1. Time of call | After | During | After | During | After | During | During | After | After |
| 2. Source | (PC) police | Public phone 999 | Public phone 999 | Direct phone line | Direct phone line | Public phone 999 | Public phone 999 | Public phone, 7 digit | Direct phone line |
| 3. Channel | Radio | VDU | VDU | VDU | VDU | VDU | VDU | VDU | VDU |
| 4. Location of event | Place (subdivision) cells | Caller's address | Caller's address | Bus | Hospital | Caller's address (near community center) | Near home address | Home address of caller | Bus |
| 5. Caller's role | PC 107 | Citizen (observer) | Victim | Bus official | Ambulance official | Citizen (observer) | Citizen (observer) | Victim | Bus official |
| 6. Caller's location | Police subdivision cells | Caller's home | Caller's home | Bus control | Ambulance control | Caller's home | Caller's home | Caller's home | Bus control |
| 7. Persons acting | Police | Citizen | Citizen | Official | Ambulance | Citizen | Citizen | Victim | Official |
| 8. Action reported | Made an arrest | Possible stolen vehicle | Stolen van | A fight in progress | Took man to hospital | Fight | Report | Report | Reported to police |
| 9. Direction of action: toward whom or what | Man (offender) | Thief(ves)? car | Thief(ves) van | Fighters to each other | Information | Fighters to each other | Fighters to each other | Attempt to steal a car | Knifer to victim |
| 10. Descriptive term | Disorder[b] | Possible stolen vehicle | Stolen | Bus fight | Overdose of drugs | Large fight | Youths causing trouble | —[c] | Man wounded |

[a]Note that "caller's location" in the case of official calls is the ambulance, fire, or bus control and that "actions taken" and "persons acting" refer to the actions that the control center took, not the actions of the observer/participant in the event. These must, of course, be reconstructed by the controller on the basis of second-hand information relayed from the control center.
[b]In this case, "Descriptive term" refers not to the incident (arrest) but to the basis for the arrest.
[c]Data missing on records or no entry made.

## NINE INCIDENTS RECEIVED BY THE
## QUEEN'S FIELDS CONTROLLER

(1) PC radios to say that he is taking a prisoner to a jail on the subdivision (radio).

(2) VDU message from the center saying a citizen/caller thinks that a Mini Metro parked in front of a house without number plates may be stolen (999 call).

(3) VDU message from the center a man has reported a stolen van (999 call).

(4) VDU message from the center Bus Control rang the center to report a fight on a bus (direct line).

(5) VDU message from the center Ambulance Control reports that a man has been taken to hospital (direct line).

(6) VDU message from the center: woman reports a disturbance outside a community center (and her house) (999 call).

(7) VDU message from the center: man reports youths fighting outside his house (999 call).

(8) VDU message from the center: woman reports attempted theft of her vehicle (phone) (seven-digit number).

(9) VDU message: Bus Control rang the center to report a wounding aboard a bus (direct line).

The 10 syntagms shown in Table 3.1 are derived from interviews with controllers concerning the cognitive partitions they draw when focused on units within a message. This requires a projection of imagination and a framing of the unit in a possible world. The units, when taken together, form a kind of cognitive matrix that places the information within a time/space/social relations framework or set of overlapping frameworks. The event in the object world (see the rows in Figure 3.1 for these concepts) is characterized by numbers 1, 4, 5, 6, 9, and 10; the *incident*, by numbers 1, 4, 5, 6, 9, and 10; the *caller*, by numbers 3, 4, 5, 6, and 7; the *call*, by numbers 1, 2, 3, and 6; and the *actions taken*, by numbers 8 and 9. Since the incident reflects the object, there is most agreement in items bearing on both, and each is indexed by 6 of the 10 items. A different sort of operation on these syntagms or units is required if controllers are seeking to make an assignment; they will be ranked in salience (if work load dictates a priority to be set for an assignment). In this circumstance, numbers 8, 9, and 10 are used in concert with number 1 to establish the relative importance of any given assignment (this is discussed further below). However, even such rules of thumb may be altered by situational factors such as (a) a fight with prisoners in the cell, (b) the intrusion of *noise* (e.g., a malfunctioning radio/telephone or VDU), and (c) a change in social knowledge of the controller that embeds the units of a given message in broader events in the more distal social object world. If, for example, a series of bombings has taken place, a vehicle obstructing/abandoned (19 in Figure 3.2) becomes a high priority bit of information, and the assignment becomes top priority regardless of current work activities; an abandoned car may contain a bomb. These surrounding understandings can radically alter the salience and relevance of given units to the assignment process. The units are not of equal weight in naming the nature of the police problem. Furthermore, they can be altered in salience by a variety of variably relevant circumstances. These 10 items form a perceptual grid by which controllers order the world represented in the incidents they process, but it should be emphasized that the organization of the relevances of units is based on a focus upon the signs in the network that is a communicational unit. Several items, depending on the focus, can be seen to refer to the object world, to the incident, or to previously constituted items in the message-call as incident (numbers 1 and 6, for example) and are both referential (designating objects in the social world) and autoreferential (referring to themselves as aspects of a communicational unit). Furthermore, the incident selectively contains features of the event and call and so illustrates a kind of intertextuality or texts that can be seen within a text.

*Associative Context (Paradigm).* The incidents listed in Table 3.1 can be seen as a sequence linked by proximity (each is like the previous incident, and like the next incident, in several respects, e.g., it is a call with relevance to the police, it contains a time, source, and channel) or a syntagmatic/metonymic chain. On the other hand, the incidents can be clustered into groups because features of the incidents (the content of given items) or the incident as a message or whole are similar or can be associated using a context. By *context* is meant aspects of knowledge that are assumed by speakers but that may not explicitly be verbalized in the utterance (or communicational unit) (see Levinson, 1983, ch. 2). The context is the tacit or unseen basis for handling or processing calls. Given a syntagm, one can place it in any number of associative contexts, and how to do this, and what such a placement means, is not taught to police, nor is it written down anywhere for their reference. These are learned ways of connecting expression and content, and grouping various signs so composed into meaningful action-units. It is a kind of mental sorting and classification that one does everyday, but it is crucial to understand it in this organization, because it is the basis on which the police are mobilized and take action.

There are at least five of these associative contexts. They will not be fully described, nor will examples be provided, because this would require detailed exposition, and an integration of fieldwork knowledge, technical knowledge, semiotic knowledge, and knowledge of British culture. To some degree, these are not mutually exclusive, and may be used together. The context within which a call is placed may change, or the officer may retain it "in his head" until he decides what sorts of action to take. This is mental and interpretative work that places a few bits of information, "facts," into a context that permits organizational action to be directed. The first context is *action* calls, and these contrast with calls that do not require action (e.g., ones that are filed, such as the location of road works on the subdivision), or ones that may be attended if the controller wishes to send someone (a road accident). *Events* may be placed in another context with two subcontexts, *ongoing* or *completed*. A third context is whether the *incident* in the police VDU is ongoing or completed (the incident is the organizational record, while the event is what is happening in the social world). A fourth context is *crime* versus *noncrime* calls. This may be done on the basis of the name given the incident or the controllers' own judgment about the report. A fifth context is the controller's *imagination of the event*, and his or her *reconstruction* of what was done or should be done by officers on the scene. Since the controller is given little information, he or she has to imagine what happened prior to an incident, during it, and after in order to keep records up to date. He or she must do this for both closed and open incident files.

## MININARRATIVES

These incidents, or transformed calls as messages, possess an apparent structure, order, and coherence. They are, as it were, *mininarratives*, or stories. To state that an incident is a collapsed narrative or mininarrative is to assume the operations underlying them and to gloss them as well for the purposes of analysis. The narrative structure thus contains within it a host of richly contextualized meanings, imputed understandings, and expectations of reactions that are used to make sensible the incidents as read. The context of "ongoing incident," however, forms them as stories of a particular type, providing an unfolding line of action, a set of characters and plot, central peripheral actions, and outcomes. These stories can be rendered or reordered to produce simpler and yet more abstract relational patterns (see Propp, 1958; Rumelhart, 1975).

In the analysis that follows, it is shown that incidents' stories possess a narrative structure based upon the actions of the central figures as seen from the modality or voice of the police or the third party. There is a protagonist, mutually affecting actions and conditions upon that action. The unit of analysis is the incident. The event or the central crucible transforms the hero and the others through interaction, while the police play something of an unfinished metahero role. Using the material in Table 3.2, we can attempt to reduce some features of these stories further.

Preliminarily, we map the nine calls used as exemplars of the approach into a grid of types of incidents that are in turn transformed events (reported by citizens or officials to police operators who then send them on). The caller's role may be indexed by a mere voice on an automatic alarm or the call of an official of a company. These represent surrogate victims. An individual victim or an observer of someone else's plight may call. These can be coded as victim (person or organization) or observer as shown in Table 3.2. The target of the action reported in the incident about the event can be either an official or a citizen. These three axes when combined describe types of incidents or associative contexts for assembling texts. The axes are the principal causal concerns of the controller.

Each of the calls/incidents can be thus typed using the pattern of present or absent attributes given the information known and its construction by the controller. Further subtypes could be produced if a larger number of calls were to be analyzed. These incidents demonstrate a specialized body of knowledge and interpretation of human behavior. They contain a set of figures, motives, expected outcomes, and moral implications.

Table 3.2 shows aspects of the cognitive substructuring of common-sense police knowledge in regard to these types of calls on this subdivision. It might be noted that like the idea of "text" or "syntagm," what is believed to be known about such events in the object-world, is always surrounded by a set of understood but not stated premises. Barthes (1977) terms these "indices," or characteristics assumed or repressed, not a part of the encoding of the text. The role of elevating of these meanings while suppressing others is played by organizational coding and interpretation.

**Table 3.2.** Incident Types Arrayed by Event, Actors, Targets, and Call Sources as Seen by Controllers

| Incident Type | Action in the Event | Target in the Event | Call Source |
|:---:|:---:|:---:|:---:|
| 1 | + | + | + |
| 2 | + | + | – |
| 3 | + | 0 | + |
| 4 | + | 0 | – |
| 5 | + | – | – |
| 6 | + | – | + |
| 7 | – | – | – |
| 8 | – | 0 | + |
| 9 | – | + | + |
| 10 | – | – | + |
| 11 | – | 0 | – |
| 12 | – | + | – |
| | + = Victim (person or organization) | + = Person | + = Official |
| | – = Observer | – = Property 0 = Social Order | – = Citizen |

*NOTE: A minus means the target was property and *not* social order, *not* a person.

Each of these types is a summated story. It captures the subject of the event, the object of the event, the observer (victim), the villain, their implicit action sequences (observed car was missing, checked memory for where last parked, rang police, requested that they come) and the implicit hero or metahero (the police). Type 5 (+––) victim of property offense (stolen car) rings police, type 8 (–++) observer of personal offense rings bus control, bus control rings police, and type 10 (–0–) observer of order event (or possible personal offense) rings police.

These narrative substructures are very crude extractions from a large set of influences. Analysis of additional calls might produce a set of subtypes of villain, for example, or callers by motive or more complex action sequences. But it is likely that screening at this point is quite general and gross, and such nuances are merely incidental to the work rather than essential.

All the calls are mapped from the police perspective or modality; it can be assumed that citizens may view the syntactical structure of events rather differently. The combinations suggested in this preliminary analysis such as the relations between hero, villain(s), metahero, target, and subject within a police story with an ongoing plot, story line, climax, and resolution require a much more detailed analysis with additional data as well as an expanded conceptual framework to illustrate them properly (see Scholes and Kellogg, 1966).

It would appear that the sequence of events discussed here is a partial rendition of stages one, two, and three in an expanded narrative. For example, a sequence of the following kind might be imagined:

(1) Preliminaries (argument, plan, fight, car stolen)
(2) Crime event (various sorts)
(3) Event reported to officials (police, and so on)
(4) Investigation (uniformed branch, CID, specialist squad[s]
(5) Resolution (closed investigation, court, clearance or crime, and so on)

Not all empirical events will progress through all the stages listed, the order may not follow this precisely, and some of the stages may overlap each other. This is the bare outline of a formal model of the resolution of a police story. Even the absence of a stage is, of course, significant, and truncated stories, collapsed sequences, and "failed" or incomplete stories may have importance for elaborating the model and explicating the possible connection between narrative structure, catharsis, and shaping the experience of everyday life.

The analysis of texts that draws on narrative structure of police stories also draws upon general knowledge of plays, television, novels, fairy tales, and traditional folktales. Police stories are a particular copy of everyday life; any copy risks being bogus, false, deceptive, and intrusive in social reality that is not so marked and framed. In one sense, police stories represent a reversal of nature or of narratives of everyday life; they are rather a copy of nature, in this case, defined as culture. Thus the modeling of everyday life in the text of a police incident and of police narratives should be examined not for veracity or irony, but rather as a specially framed bit of culture (see Barley, 1983).

### SEMIOSIS

*Semiosis*, the growth and change in meaning of signs, is perhaps the most difficult process to exemplify, and the most controversial, so only a few examples will be used here to illustrate it. Three different sorts of semiosis can be illustrated. The first is change in meaning that results from the layering of denotative meaning with connotative or more implicit meaning. For example, in the MPD, when a call comes to the operator, she classifies it (gives it a number): Each number is on one hand a label for a kind of event (burglary, robbery, car theft), and on the other, the basis for a priority (first, second, or third). These are denotative meanings, specified by the operator when she creates a file for a call and thus makes an incident. The operator also attaches connotative meaning to a call (another way of stating this is to say that the calls are placed within several associative contexts). Examples of this are associations such as it being crime or noncrime, requiring EMS (emergency medical service) or not, and the fact that each call is work, or produces necessary task-related actions by the operator such as making a file, using the phone to alert an area controller (in the next room) who will be transmitting the call to a car for attention, and sending the incident on to the zone controller's printer. This form of semiosis means that for any given message, the facts are constituted in different fashion and have different implications. A second form of semiosis comes about as the message moves from one location in the organization to another. For example, the denotative meanings of a call now an incident are the same for operators and zone controllers (classification, crime/noncrime, priority) and their connotative meanings, "work," are also analogous; the meaning of the message changes very little between those two locations. But the officers, the third location, classify their jobs or assignments using the same three denotative meanings, but also sort assignments into those with an honorable potential (a chance to do some good police work) or not. This connotative meaning adds a potential for competition with other officers, stealing and "jumping" calls (taking a call directed to another unit and trying to be the first on the scene to make the arrest, apprehend the suspect, and so on), and lying. Change in meaning of the call leads to changes in behavior that differentiate one organizational segment from two others. Honorable calls are those that lead to prestige within the department, such as arrest, and/or those that do not associate the officer with drunks, domestic disputes, or time-consuming paperwork. A third form of semiosis is the general reduction in the relevant number of data points as one moves from the front to the back of the system. Operators possess quite a lot of information in both the BPD and the MPD, but condense, chunk, and code it until only the items stated in the format are used. Zone controllers received a preformatted message with a few select points of interest, such as time, address, nature of the event, priority, and they in turn condense and summarize the incident into a few words "1859 Woodward Ave. fight on premises." In formal terms, the level of information drops, but implicit or tacit meanings (connotative) increase and surround and embed the message. It has been argued that one consequence of message processing is the production of *drama* (Manning, 1982b). In one fashion, the messages can be said to become more poetic, as they are more self-referential and reflexive in character; they are overlaid with connotative meanings not derived from the nature of the call nor the caller's intentions; and they selectively highlight certain features of the call as it becomes revealed as a job.

The piling, one upon the other, of meanings, and their layering within the PCS, is done through connections within and across domains, all bound by the invisible envelope of the occupational culture (Manning, 1982a). This envelope is itself a context that is only occasionally examined, but it operates to give order to the transmissions or messages through subsystems. The extent of compatibility between and among other domains that might have been chosen is not known.

One of the difficult questions that arises from the analysis of chains of signification is that of what the *message* is. In some sense, the message is a text, or a prediction of the various ways of reading off texts in the three subsystems. In another way, it disappears when one sees it as a mere object coming under the control of a system of signs. If messages are defined in terms of semiotic structures, then they so exist or not at all (Eco, 1979b, p. 316). They dissolve as independent entities and reappear as occasions for coding. It has been argued in the previous sections that not only do messages change in their form as they move through the system, but they also change in their meaning. As the message moves physically through the system, it moves metaphorically as well. The microcosm of the controller's decisions represents a subsystem within the organization in which changes in meaning occur over time. If one focuses on the *semanitic consequences* of the processing of messages, it is probably not fruitful to view it as transformation, because that would connote something more formal than what is in fact taking place.

## Summary

This chapter contains data and analysis gathered from two studies carried out relying on fieldwork and utilizing semiotics as an analytic tool. Some of the examples were drawn from the study of policing in Britain, some from studies done in the United States. One study is based upon conceptions of policy within a British Governmental Inspectorate (or "regulatory agency" as it might be called in America). The examples were put in a sequence to illustrate movement from somewhat complex to more complex concepts, and to show how facets of this progression are intimately related. The more subtle questions of diachronic, or temporally patterned, analysis must necessarily build upon the established units and contexts, and questions of organizational analysis are dependent upon a detailed understanding of stabilized and conventionalized meanings as well as more volatile and changing meanings.

## NOTES

1. The research reported here is funded in part by a grant to the Socio-Legal Centre, Wolfson College, Oxford, for the period 1983-1987. Interviews and observations were gathered between July 1984 and July 1985.
2. From Manning (1986b).
3. Site: a known location such as Woolworth's or the Boar's Head Pub; place: corner of Mayfair and Poole Roads; address: 124 Junction Road; other: on a vehicle, a moving affray.

## 4. REFLECTIONS

The brevity of this volume makes conclusion and/or summary rather redundant. The overview provided here summarizes the key points made in the previous three chapters, with special emphasis upon the integration of fieldwork and semiotics. The claim is that issues of primary importance to fieldworkers, such as their role relations in the field, in particular the types of roles they play, the sorts of accommodations they make to field situations, and the affects that these might have on data gathering and analysis, reflect the somewhat limited uses to which fieldwork has been put. In the remainder of the chapter, fieldwork's strengths and weaknesses and overall aims are related to the limitations of fieldwork in a broader perspective, not simply within the world of assumed problems to which fieldworkers typically address their attention. The orientation of semiotics and some of the principles and examples presented in Chapter 3 are reviewed and provide the backdrop for a discussion about the complementarity of fieldwork and semiotics.

As shown in Chapter 1, fieldwork has focused on a handful of issues that arise from its central concern or aim, which is to establish a relationship within the field such that data can be obtained. These have included a concern with the background, aims, and sponsorship of the observer; the roles of observers, especially whether they are overt or covert; the tactics and strategies of penetrating another alien culture; the pressures (social, psychological, and practical) to conform to the host culture in ways that somewhat alter one's data-gathering and analysis aims; the types of data gathered; the role of openness in producing mutual confidence and trust and ultimately in enhancing the quality of the data and the degree and type of identification with one's subjects, people, hosts, or those with whom one has shared secrets. Fieldwork, as a naturalistic, descriptive enterprise, seeks for the most part to gain a deep understanding of culture as members might see it. Some alternatives to fieldwork have sought to specify and formalize traditions exemplified in the works of Agar, Wallace, Goodnenough, Metzger, Romney, and Frake, but the limits of fieldwork as a theoretic and analytic enterprise are related to its strengths.

Chapter 1 showed that the five features of fieldwork were particularly limiting with respect to creating generalizable knowledge. The problems chosen for analysis are based on individual opportunities, in part because fieldwork is inexpensive, easy for a single person to carry out, and full of powerful and rewarding experience for those involved. Fieldwork, even team-based fieldwork, focuses on a narrow domain of knowledge within a broader cultural framework. In spite of the concern with role relations in the field, it is fairly obvious that the *actual* relations fieldworkers develop vary widely, and that it is extremely difficult to determine how such role relations affect(ed) their data. The descriptive focus of ethnography is reflected in the focus of fieldwork, but the fit is not a necessary one. It is possible to undertake analytically focused fieldwork to test hypotheses derived from field studies or from sample surveys. Finally, with few exceptions, fieldworkers do not use explicitly comparative methods, and often focus on a single people, tribe, or neighborhood.

Semiotics proceeds from a formal model of language and language use. Although there are debates about the degree to which language models the world, whether the science of signs is ultimately a science of verbal signs that becomes an analogue for nonverbal sign systems (Barthes, 1973), or whether the science of signs is ultimately referential (concerned with objects in the world) or merely auto-referential (a closed system such as mathematics that has reference in any known everyday world), it is a formal and rational model-building and model-based approach. The generalized model guides the selection of problems as well as the comparative methodology. The subjective or emotive aspect of communication has a somewhat problematic role in semiotics, for it is included in Jakobson's model of communication, but is often omitted by others who focus entirely on the rules, forms, codes, and texts, and within a single domain such as law (see Jackson, 1985). One of the most difficult of all issues for semiotics is that of context, or those matters of understanding brought to a message by the hearer and the speaker. This is true for any sign system. For example, an advertisement for Honda based on the porcine face of a silly-acting adolescent loses some of its cachet if the viewer does not know that this man is Jim MacMahon, the quarterback of the Chicago Bears football team, hero of the Super Bowl, and commercial savant.

The tension between building formal models such as the mininarratives discussed in Chapter 3 and the empirical facts of messages to the police, their diversity, emotional quality, and their spatial and temporal distribution in the social world, remains. A semiotic focus upon codes, rules, and principles will stand in contrast to an analysis of encodation, interpretation, semiosis, and changes in meaning and interpretation (Jameson, 1972).

In Chapter 3, six broad principles of semiotics were presented and their relationship to fieldwork outlined. These included the idea that semiotics provides a means of identifying problem areas for fieldworkers prior to undertaking fieldwork; assists in the systematic search for units of analysis and the context within which these operate; provides a means for formalizing analysis more generally; requires comparisons and a comparative method; makes the search for analytic models underlying surface meanings or the concrete features of everyday life necessary; and assumes differing perspectives on social life. The weaknesses of such a set of principles are that they may strip ethnographic analysis of the rich description and complexity that is a basis for all sociological analysis, that they will encourage a kind of premature closure on field problems and reward pseudoformalism, which overlooks the complexity of such fundamental concepts as opposition, reversal, and duality—the geometry of social life. It may also miss the value of formal models and techniques: to highlight what cannot be explained by such approaches. What is omitted or remains implicit in any explanation? If one is focused on forms of discourse that communicate the law, what are the social and cultural aspects of the context in which law operates? For any social organization, are there not several models used to imagine the social roles, the technology, the interpretations used (Manning, 1979)? How does one decide between these explanations if they differ? How do codes change?

The implications of this book for the study of everyday life more generally have only been alluded to in the previous chapters. The relevance of formal modes of analysis is not simply a theoretic one. There are aspects of modern society that suggest that two currents are adrift. The first is the directionless and hedonistic features of American society. For example—the absence of silence and the fear of privacy, some of which is captured on Lasch's book, the *Culture of Narcissism* (1978). The reduced formalism in many aspects of life is suggested by the absence of differentiation of the graduation ceremony (above) from everyday life. A variety of other little cues suggests this as well. I take in no order of importance: the wearing of hats (workingman's baseball-type caps with Rainbird, Budweiser, Strohs, or Richard's Body Shop on the front) inside and out and as a part of the head rather than as a bit of clothing to be tipped; the reduced prevalence of rituals of marriage such as engagement, and marriage itself as a ceremonial-ritual matter; the decline of greetings into "hi" and "have a good one"; the conflation of television news, sports, and weather into a comedy panel of clowns trading commentary; the deterioration of formal dress and knowledge of manners generally; and the emphasis upon feeling, "concerns," weight, shape, appearance, and material acquisition above form, etiquette, restraint, and tradition of any kind.

On the other hand, the interstices of life are being formalized almost without full knowledge. The computerization of virtually all billing and monetary transactions means a built-in paradox of personal service and mechanical and formal constraint. For example, I had been in England for almost a year and had not used my Michigan Magic Money card during that time. I had the card and my "personal identification number," I inserted the card in December of 1984, and the screen lighted with a small Christmas tree made from x's:

It then flashed, after I had put in my number, "Merry Christmas, Peter Manning." I was pleased; it had remembered me and wanted my business! I requested $50.00. It replied, unhelpfully, "Transaction cannot be completed" and did this several more times (Christmas Carols were being played via Muzak in the Magic Money Booth). I left and went to another booth to try my luck there (I thought perhaps the machine was out of money). I failed at two other stations and gave up. I went into the bank the following day and they told me, of course, that my number had been "deactivated" because I had not used the card in the last six months. Personal service. Formal language overwhelms us. A supermarket clerk tells a woman who says she is learning to drive, that because she does not have a drivers' license she cannot write a check. "We have to have something we can program into our computer," she says. Clerks at airline terminals cannot assign a seat, even when they have a plan behind them on a large map from which they pull seat numbers when the computer is "down." Contradictions arise because items cannot be sold because the computer will not accept the automatic code on the item, or it is overloaded. Computers provide a *mediating* force in everyday life, producing contradictions between face-to-face encounters and relationships and formal programs, bills, procedures, and deadlines. People can now communicate by computers, using them as answering machines and secretaries, and call-forwarding devices. We adopt the language of machines to describe emotions. Much has been written about the notion of reification, of giving thinglike status to ideas and concepts. The more worrying is the omnipresent *pathetic fallacy*: giving things, machines, and inanimate objects the status of feeling beings. A complementary process is treating people as machines, or the *mechanistic fallacy*. We love our things and use people, as Fromm warned would happen. Thus the advertising on television sells urgently the most useless of objects (hair dye, tiny deodorant pads, water flavored with sugar) and screams with joy about the most banal such as beer and cars. Relations are seen through material objects.

Formalization erodes feeling, and replaces it with constructed, artificial, commercialized feelings, desires, and needs of the market (Barthes, 1972). It is not surprising that the growth of formalism comes as a way of replacing other sorts of ordering notions: values, beliefs, religions, even national sovereignty. It provides a form of certainty in uncertain worlds. Is this an analogue to the growth of pseudoformalism in the shape of the computerization of society (Nora and Minc, 1981)?

The two cross-cutting modes of decreasing and increasing formalization operate at different levels, one more covert and the other overt and in part a response to the covert formalization of large numbers of exchange transactions. It may be that in order to study the technological destruction of forms of social relationships, we must begin to see how social relations are shaped by technology and how technology provides a model for social relations in a pragmatic and technology-driven society such as America (see Bittner, 1983).

# REFERENCES

Adler, P. A. 1985. *Wheeling and Dealing*. New York: Columbia University Press.

Adler, P. and P. Adler. 1987. *Membership Roles in Field Research*. Newbury Park, CA: Sage.

Agar, M. 1985. *Speaking of Ethnography*. Newbury Park, CA: Sage.

Altheide, D. 1976. *Creating Reality*. Newbury Park, CA: Sage.

Atkinson, J. M. and J. Heritage, eds. 1985. Structures of Social Action. Cambridge: Cambridge University Press.

Barley, S. 1983. "Semiotics and the Study of Organizational and Occupational Cultures." *ASQ* 28(September):393-413.

Barthes, R. 1972. *Mythologies*. New York: Hill and Wang.

Barthes, R. 1975. *The Pleasures of the Text*. New York: Hill and Wang.

Barthes, R. 1977. *Image/Music/Text*. New York: Hill and Wang.

Bateson, G. 1972. *Steps Toward an Ecology of Mind*. San Francisco: Chandler.

Becker, H. S. 1970. *Sociological Work*. Chicago: Aldine.

Becker, H. S. 1982. *Art Worlds*. Berkeley: University of California Press.

Becker, H. S., B. Geer, E. C. Hughes, and A. Strauss. 1961. *Boys in White*. Chicago: University of Chicago Press.

Bernstein, B. 1971. *Class, Codes, and Control. Vol. 1: Theoretical Studies Towards a Sociology of Language*. London: Routledge & Kegan Paul.

Berreman, G. 1962. *Behind Many Masks*. New York: Applied Anthropology Association Monographs.

Berreman, G. 1966. "Anemic and Etic Analyses in Social Anthropology." *American Anthropologist* 68:346-354.

Bittner, E. 1983. "Technique and the Conduct of Life." *Social Problems* 30(February):249-261.

Blumer, H. 1958. "Race Prejudice as a Sense of Group Position." *Pacific Sociological Review* 1:3-7.

Blumer, H. 1969. *Symbolic Interactionism*. Englewood Cliffs, NJ: Prentice-Hall.

Boon, J. 1982. *Other Tribes, Other Scribes*. Cambridge: Cambridge University Press.

Brown, R. 1963. *Explanation in Social Science*. Chicago: Aldine.

Brown, R. and M. Ford. 1961. "Address in American English." *Journal of Abnormal Social Psychology* 62:375-385.

Bruyn, S. 1966. *The Human Perspective in Sociology*. Englewood Cliffs, NJ: Prentice-Hall.

Cahill, S. et al. 1985. "Meanwhile Backstage: Public Bathrooms and the Interaction Order." *Urban Life* 14(April):33-58.

Cicourel, A. V. 1964. *Method and Measurement in Sociology*. New York: Free Press.

Cicourel, A. V. 1973. *Cognitive Sociology*. Harmondsworth: Penguin.

74

Cicourel, A. V. 1985. "Text and Discourse." Pp. 159-185 in *Annual Review of Anthropology 14*. Palo Alto, CA: Annual Reviews, Inc.

Cressey, D. 1953. *Other People's Money*. New York: Free Press.

Culler, J. 1975. *Structuralist Poetics*. Ithaca, NY: Cornell University Press.

Dalton, M. 1959. *Men Who Manage*. New York: John Wiley.

Davis, N. J. 1975. *Sociological Constructions of Deviance*. Dubuque: W. C. Brown.

Denzin, N. 1978. *The Research Act*. New York: McGraw-Hill.

Derrida, J. 1976. *On Grammatology*, translated (with a preface) by Gayatri Chakravorty Spivak. Baltimore: Johns Hopkins University Press.

Douglas, J. D. 1967. *The Social Meanings of Suicide*. Princeton, NJ: Princeton University Press.

Douglas, J. D. 1971. *American Social Order*. New York: Free Press.

Douglas, J. D. 1976. *Investigative Social Research*. Newbury Park, CA: Sage.

Douglas, J. D. and J. Johnson, eds. 1977. *Existential Sociology*. New York: Cambridge University Press.

Douglas, M. 1970. *Natural Symbols*. New York: Pantheon.

Douglas, M. 1980. *Evans-Pritchard*. London: Fontana/Collins.

Eco, U. 1979a. *The Role of the Reader*. Bloomington: University of Indiana Press.

Eco, U. 1979b. *A Theory of Semiotics*. Bloomington: University of Indiana Press.

Eco, U. 1984. *Semiotics and the Philosophy of Language*. London: Macmillan.

Emerson, R. M., ed. 1983. *Contemporary Field Research*. Boston: Little, Brown.

Epstein, A. L., ed. 1967. *The Craft of Anthropology*. London: Tavistock.

Fabrega, H., Jr. 1974. *Disease and Social Behavior*. Cambridge: MIT Press.

Faunce, W. A. 1984. "School Achievement, Social Status and Self-Esteem." *Social Psychology Quarterly* 47(1):3-14.

Fowler, R. 1977. *Linguistics and the Novel*. London: Methuen.

Frake, C. 1961. "Diagnosis of Disease Among the Subannum of Mindanao." *American Anthropologist* 63:113-132.

Fussell, P. 1980. *Abroad: British Literary Travelers Between the Wars*. Oxford: Oxford University Press.

Garfinkel, H. 1967. *Studies in Ethnomethodology*. Englewood Cliffs, NJ: Prentice-Hall.

Garfinkel, H. and H. Sacks. 1970. "On Formal Structures of Practical Actions." Pp. 338-366 in *Theoretical Sociology*, edited by J. C. McKinney and E. A. Tiryakian. New York: Appleton-Century-Crofts.

Geertz, C. 1973. *The Interpretation of Culture*. New York: Basic Books.

Geertz, C. 1983. *Local Knowledge*. New York: Basic Books.

Geertz, C. 1985. "The State of Anthropology." *London Times Literary Supplement* (November).

Glaser, B. and A. Strauss. 1967. *The Discovery of Grounded Theory*. Chicago: Aldine.

Gluckman, M. 1971. *Analysis of a Social Situation in Modern Zulu Land*. Rhodes-Livingstone Papers #28. Manchester: Manchester University Press.

Godelier, M. 1977. *Perspectives in Marxist Anthropology*, translated by R. Brain. Cambridge: Cambridge University Press.

Goffman, E. 1959. *The Presentation of Self in Everyday Life*. Garden City, NY: Doubleday Anchor Books.

Goffman, E. 1961. *Asylums*. Chicago: Aldine.

Goffman, E. 1967. *Encounters*. Indianapolis: Bobbs-Merrill.

Goffman, E. 1969. *Strategic Interaction*. Philadelphia: University of Pennsylvania.

Goffman, E. 1972. *Relations in Public*. New York: Basic Books.

Goffman, E. 1974. *Frame Analysis*. Cambridge, MA: Harvard University Press.

Goffman, E. 1981. *Forms of Talk*. Oxford: Basil Blackwell.

Guiraud, P. 1975. *Semiology*. London: Routledge & Kegan Paul.

Haas, J. and W. Shaffer. 1984. "The 'Fate of Idealism' Revisited." *Urban Life* 13(April):63-81.

Halliday, M.A.K. 1978. *Language as a Social Semiotic*. London: Edward Arnold.

Hammersley, M. and P. Atkinson. 1983. *Ethnography*. New York: Tavistock.

Handel, W. 1982. *Ethnomethodology*. Englewood Cliffs, NJ: Prentice-Hall.

Hawkes, T. 1977. *Structuralism and Semiotics*. Berkeley: University of California Press.

Heritage, J. 1985. *Garfinkel and Ethnomethodology*. Oxford: Polity Press.

Hughes, E. C. 1971. *The Sociological Eye*. Chicago: Aldine.

Hunter, Floyd. 1960. *Community Power Structure*. Chapel Hill: University of North Carolina Press.

Jackson, B. 1985. *Semiotics and Legal Theory*. London: Routledge & Kegan Paul.

Jakobson, R. 1960. "Linguistics and Poetics." Pp. 350-377 in *Style in Language*, edited by T. Sebeok. Cambridge: MIT Press.

Jameson, F. 1972. *The Prison-House of Language*. Princeton, NJ: Princeton University Press.

Johnson, J. 1975. *Doing Fieldwork*. New York: Free Press.

Junker, B., ed. 1960. *Fieldwork: An Introduction to the Social Sciences*. Chicago: University of Chicago Press.

Kearns, K. 1981. "Urban Squatter Strategy." *Urban Life* 10(July):123-153.

Knorr-Cetina, K. 1981. *The Manufacture of Knowledge*. Oxford: Pergamon.

Kotarba, J. and A. Fontana, eds. 1984. *The Existential Self in Society*. Chicago: University of Chicago Press.

Kristeva, J. 1981. *Desire in Language*. New York: Columbia University Press.

Kurzweil, E. 1980. *The Age of Structuralism*. New York: Columbia University Press.

Lasch, Christopher. 1978. *The Culture of Narcissism*. New York: Norton.

Leach, E. R. 1976. *Culture and Communication*. Cambridge: Cambridge University Press.

Leiter, K. 1980. *Primer on Ethnomethodology*. New York: Oxford University Press.

Lemert, C. 1979a. *Sociology and the Twilight of Man: Homocentrism and Discourse in Sociological Theory*. Carbondale: Southern Illinois University Press.

Lemert, C. 1979b. "Structuralist Semiotics." Pp. 96-111 in *Theoretical Sociology*, edited by S. G. McNall. New York: St. Martin's Press.

Levinson, S. 1983. *Pragmatics*. Cambridge: Cambridge University Press.

Lilly, R. and R. A. Ball. 1981. "No-Tell Motel: The Management of Social Invisibility." *Urban Life* 10(July):179-198.

Lofland, J. 1976. *Doing Social Life*. New York: John Wiley.

Lofland, J. and L. Lofland. 1983. *Analyzing Social Settings*. Belmont, CA: Wadsworth.

Lynch, M. 1985. *Art and Artifact in Laboratory Science*. Boston: Routledge & Kegan Paul.

Manning, P. K. 1977. *Police Work: The Social Organization of Policing*. Cambridge: MIT Press.

Manning, P. K. 1978. "Social Groups and Social Structure." Pp. 188-209 in *Sociology: The Basic Concepts*, edited by Edward Sagarin. New York: Holt, Rinehart & Winston.

Manning, P. K. 1979. "The Social Control of Police Work." Pp. 41-65 in *British Police*, edited by S. Holdaway. London: Edward Arnold.

76

Manning, P. K. 1980. *The Narcs' Game*. Cambridge: MIT Press.

Manning, P. K. 1982a. "Analytic Induction." Pp. 273-302 in *Social Science Methods. Vol. 1: Qualitative Methodology*, edited by R. B. Smith and P. K. Manning. New York: Irvington Press.

Manning, P. K. 1982b. "Organisational Work: The Enstructuration of the Environment." *British Journal of Sociology* 33(March):118-139.

Manning, P. K. 1984. "Police Classification of the Mentally Ill." Pp. 177-198 in *Mental Health and Criminal Justice*, edited by L. Teplin. Newbury Park, CA: Sage.

Manning, P. K. 1985a. "Comparative Genius" [Review Essay of R. Needham's *Against the Tranquility of Axioms*]. *American Journal of Sociology* 9(November):687-695.

Manning, P. K. 1985b. "Limits of the Semiotic Structuralist Perspective upon Organizational Analysis." Pp. 79-111 in *Studies in Symbolic Interaction*, edited by N. Denzin. Greenwich, CT: JAI Press.

Manning, P. K. 1986a. "Marketing a Self" [Review of Patricia Adler's *Wheeling and Dealing*]. *Contemporary Sociology* 15(July):507-509.

Manning, P. K. 1986b. "Signwork." *Human Relations* 39(4):283-308.

Manning, P. K. 1986c. "Texts as Echoes." *Human Studies* 9:287-302.

Manning, P. K. In press. *Signifying Calls: Organizing a Police Response*.

Manning, P. K. and H. Fabrega, Jr. 1976. "Fieldwork and the New Ethnography." *Man (n.s.)* 11(March):39-52.

Matza, David. 1969. *Becoming Deviant*. Englewood Cliffs, NJ: Prentice-Hall.

McCall, G. and J. L. Simmons, eds. 1969. *Issues in Participant Observation*. Reading, MA: Addison-Wesley.

Mehan, H. and H. Wood. 1975. *The Reality of Ethnomethodology*. New York: John Wiley.

Metzger, D. and G. Williams. 1963. "Tenejapa Medicine: The Curer." *Southwestern Journal of Anthropology* 19:216-234.

Metzger, D. and G. Williams. 1966. "Some Procedures and Results in the Study of Native Categories: Tzeltal 'Firewood.'" *American Anthropologist* 68:389-407.

Meyer, J. and C. Rowan. 1977. "Institutionalized Organizations: Formal Structure as Myth and Ceremony." *American Journal of Sociology* 83(October):340-363.

Minsky, M., ed. 1968. *Semantic Information Processing*. Cambridge: MIT Press.

Needham, R. 1978. *Primordial Characters*. Charlottesville: University Press of Virginia.

Needham, R. 1980. *Reconaissances*. Toronto: University of Toronto Press.

Needham, R. 1981. *Circumstantial Deliveries*. Berkeley: University of California Press.

Needham, R. 1983. *Against the Tranquility of Axioms*. Berkeley: University of California Press.

Needham, R. 1984. *Exemplars*. Berkeley: University of California Press.

Nora, S. and A. Minc. 1981. *The Computerization of Society*. Cambridge: MIT Press.

Park, R. E. and E. W. Burgess. 1969. *An Introduction to the Science of Sociology*. Chicago: University of Chicago Press [original work published 1921].

Park, R. L. 1973. "Life History." *American Journal of Sociology* 79:251-260.

Pettit, P. 1977. *The Concept of Structuralism*. Berkeley: University of California Press.

Pickering, A. 1985. *Constructing Quarks*. Chicago: University of Chicago Press.

Propp, V. 1958. *The Morphology of the Folk Tale*. Austin: University of Texas Press.

Redfield, R. 1941. *The Folk Culture of Yucatan*. Chicago: University of Chicago Press.

Redfield, R. 1960. *The Little Community*. Chicago: University of Chicago Press.

Robey, David, ed. 1973. *Structuralism*. Oxford: Oxford University Press.

Rock, P. 1979. *Symbolic Interactionism*. Totowa, NJ: Rowman and Littlefield.

Rumelhart, R. 1975. "Notes for a Schema for Stories." Pp. 211-236 in *Representation and Understanding: Studies in Cognitive Science*, edited by D. Bogrow and A. Collins. New York: Academic Press.

de Saussure, F. 1966. *Course in General Linguistics*, edited by C. Bally and A. Sechehaye in collaboration with A. Reidlinger; translated by W. Baskin. New York: McGraw-Hill.

Schatzman, L. and A. Strauss. 1973. *Field Research: Strategies for a Natural Sociology*. Englewood Cliffs, NJ: Prentice-Hall.

Scholes, A. R. and C. Kellogg. 1966. *The Nature of Narrative*. New York: Oxford University Press.

Schwartz, H. and J. Jacobs. 1979. *Qualitative Sociology*. New York: Free Press.

Shaw, C. K. 1931. *The Natural History of a Delinquent Career*. Chicago: University of Chicago Press.

Shaw, C. K. 1966. *The Jackroller: A Delinquent Boy's Own Story*. Chicago: University of Chicago Press [original work published 1930].

Short, J. F., ed. 1971. *The Social Fabric of the Metropolis*. Chicago: University of Chicago Press.

Spadley, J. 1979. *The Ethnographic Interview*. New York: Holt, Rinehart & Winston.

Spadley, J. 1980. *Participant Observation*. New York: Holt, Rinehart & Winston.

Sturrock, J., ed. 1979. *Structuralism and Since*. Oxford: Oxford University Press.

Suttles, G. 1968. *Social Order of the Slum*. Chicago: University of Chicago Press.

Thomas, J. 1983. "Chicago Sociology" and "Toward a Critical Ethnography." In *Urban Life* 11 [Special Issue on the Chicago School of Ethnography], edited by J. Thomas.

Thrasher, Frederick. 1927. *The Gang*. Chicago: University of Chicago Press.

Todorov, T. 1981. *Poetics of Prose*. Ithaca: Cornell University Press.

Tyler, S., ed. 1969. *Cognitive Anthropology*. New York: Holt, Rinehart & Winston.

Unruh, D. 1985. "Personal Conceptions of Social Integration Among the Aging." *Urban Life* 14(April):95-117.

Van Maanen, J., ed. 1983. *Qualitative Methods*. Newbury Park, CA: Sage.

Van Maanen, J. In press. *Tales of the Field*.

Van Maanen, J., J. Dabbs, and R. Faulkner, eds. 1984. *Varieties of Qualitative Research*. Newbury Park, CA: Sage.

Vogt, E. Z. 1969. *Zincantan*. Cambridge, MA: Harvard University Press.

Vogt, E. Z. 1976. *Tortillas for the Gods*. Cambridge, MA: Harvard University Press.

Warner, W. L. 1960. *Yankee City*. New Haven, CT: Yale University Press.

Warren, C.A.B. and P. Rasmussen. 1977. "Sex and Gender in Field Research." - *Urban Life* 6:349-369.

Wax, M. 1972. "Tenting with Malinowski." *American Sociological Review* 37(February):1-13.

Wax, R. 1952. "Reciprocity as a Field Technique." *Human Organization* 11:34-37.

Whyte, W. F. 1955. *Street Corner Society*. Chicago: University of Chicago Press [original work published 1943].

Woolgar, S. and B. Latour. 1979. *Laboratory Life*. Newbury Park, CA: Sage.

## ABOUT THE AUTHOR

PETER K. MANNING (M.A. 1963, Ph.D. 1966, Duke; M.A. 1982, Oxon) specializes in phenomenological analyses of complex social systems within subfields of criminology and medical sociology. He is currently Professor of Sociology and Psychiatry at Michigan State University. He has taught or held positions at the University of Missouri; Michigan State; SUNY, Albany; MIT; the Centre for Socio-Legal Studies, Wolfson College, Oxford; and Balliol College, Oxford. He has published a number of books, articles, and chapters, including *Police Work* (1977) and *Narcs' Game* (1980), and is the author of the forthcoming *Signifying Calls*. For the past two years, he has been studying the regulation of nuclear power production in Britain and is preparing a book. He is also writing (with Keith Hawkins) *Legal Decision-Making*.